S0-ACC-047

Presented to:

From:

On the occasion of:

RACING WITH GIANTS

Copyright © 2009 by Mike Hembree

Published in Nashville, Tennessee, by Thomas Nelson®.
Thomas Nelson is a registered trademark of Thomas
Nelson, Inc.

All rights reserved. No portion of this publication may be
reproduced, stored in a retrieval system, or transmitted
by any means—electronic, mechanical, photocopying,
recording, or any other—except for brief quotations in
printed reviews, without the prior written permission of
the publisher.

Thomas Nelson, Inc. titles may be purchased in bulk for
educational, business, fund-raising, or sales promotional
use. For information, please e-mail SpecialMarkets@
ThomasNelson.com.

Unless otherwise noted, all Scripture references are from
NEW KING JAMES VERSION © 1992 by
Thomas Nelson, Inc.

Other Scripture references are taken from *New International
Version* (NIV) © 1984 by the International Bible Society.
Used by permission of Zondervan Bible Publishers; *Holy
Bible*, New Living Translation (NLT) © 1996. Used by
permission of Tyndale House Publishers, Inc., Wheaton, Ill.
All rights reserved.

Project Manager: Lisa Stilwell
Project Editor: Jessica Inman

Designed by Koechel Peterson and Associates, Inc.,
Minneapolis, Minnesota

Photography by Phil Cavali Photography. philcavali.com

Labonte 1982 (pg 107), and Earnhardt 1975 (pg 40) by
Dorsey Patrick Photography

ISBN-10: 1-4041-8701-4
ISBN-13: 978-1-4041-8701-6

Printed and bound in China

www.thomasnelson.com

09 10 11 12 [MLT] 6 5 4 3 2 1

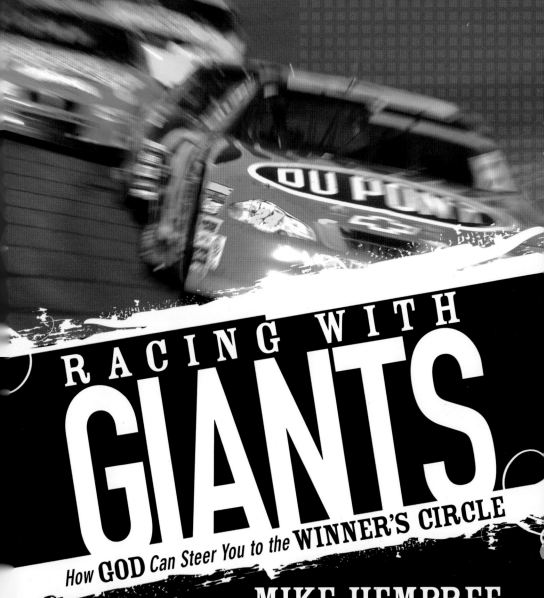

RACING WITH
GIANTS

How **GOD** Can Steer You to the **WINNER'S CIRCLE**

MIKE HEMBREE

foreword by **KYLE PETTY**

photographs provided by **PHIL CAVALI**

THOMAS NELSON
Since 1798

NASHVILLE   DALLAS   MEXICO CITY   RIO DE JANEIRO   BEIJING

TABLE OF CONTENTS

OVERCOMING LIFE'S
OBSTACLES
by KYLE PETTY

// NASCAR racing, at its very core, is a weekly examination that challenges you to overcome adversity. Very rarely do you have a perfect race. There are just too many facets to stock car racing for everything to run smoothly thirty-eight weeks of the year. Within a 500-mile race, something will inevitably happen to throw you off course, and you will need to adjust.

That same dynamic is found off the racetrack as well. God does not make things easy on you, nor should He. He provides you with the tools necessary to be successful in whatever you choose to do, but it is up to you to draw on your inner fortitude to overcome any obstacles that may stand in your way.

The same goes for every area of life. It's not whether you get knocked down—you will; it's how you get back up that defines who you are as a person. Your faith plays a large role in that. As a spiritual person, it is my belief that there is a higher being at work in everything we encounter.

As the Bible says in Proverbs 3:5–6: "Trust in the LORD with all your heart; do not depend on your own understanding. Seek his will in all you do, and he will show you which path to take" (NLT).

I have faced obstacles in both my professional and personal life. I have lost family and friends to the sport that I have devoted my life to. Many were taken from us in the prime of their life, but it was my belief that they were needed up above that helped me and my family through those times.

From one of those instances, our family has risen to impact a number of young people in a positive way. The Victory Junction Gang Camp was the brainchild of my son, Adam. Adam was taken from us in a practice accident at New Hampshire Motor Speedway in 2000. Before he died, he had envisioned a medically staffed and supported summer camp where children with terminal and life-threatening illnesses could have the opportunity to experience camp just like any other kid. We officially opened Victory Junction in his honor in 2004. When these kids leave camp, they have the same infectious smile that Adam wore, and we know that he is still part of our lives.

Without my faith, I don't know if I would have been able to pick up the pieces and finish what Adam had started. But throughout these difficult years, I know that I have become a stronger person. That's what defeating adversity is all about. If we trust God and persevere, life's hard times don't have to overcome us. We can allow adversity to make us better, stronger people.

....

Comfort and prosperity have never enriched the
world as much as adversity has.

DR. BILLY GRAHAM

Dale Earnhardt Jr.

CHAPTER one

FACING A GIANT

// **Dale Earnhardt Jr.,** the son of one of the most popular racers in NASCAR history, was just coming of age in his own racing career. But when his father was killed on the last lap of the Daytona 500 in February of 2001, Junior found his life turned upside down.

/// Earnhardt Sr. often used Junior's nickname, "June Bug," when talking about him.

START YOUR ENGINES

Begin each day with prayer asking for God's wisdom. He knows the course and sees your possible missteps. Thank Him for His care and guidance.

EARNHARDT SR. WAS AN ICON.

He had won a record seven national championships using a rough-and-tumble driving style that endeared him to millions of fans. Many thought of him almost as part of their own families because he grew up in a small North Carolina textile mill village, battling his way out of tough circumstances to success and fame.

When he died, Earnhardt's legion of fans lost a hero, and they grieved openly and publicly. Thousands traveled to Earnhardt's racing shop in Mooresville, North Carolina, to leave flowers and

DEAR GOD, I believe in You, but I'm so lost without Your help. Open my heart to Your ways. Open my ears to Your word. Help me surrender my life to You. I'm but a child struggling along the way. I want to know You, Lord. Give me Your wisdom, and bless me, I pray.

Earnhardt caps, photographs, and other memorabilia along the fence fronting the property. One fan even left his prosthetic leg—he wouldn't need it anymore, he wrote in a note, because he would no longer be traveling to watch his hero race.

FOR DALE EARNHARDT JR., THE PAIN WAS ESPECIALLY IMMENSE. RACING HAD LOST A STAR. EARNHARDT JR. HAD LOST A FATHER.

In the dizzying week that followed, Junior returned to racing only a few days after putting his father to rest. It seemed that the world suddenly sat on his shoulders, and some thought his budding driving career would dissolve.

Junior dealt with his father's death in part by facing it directly. Prior to the NASCAR circuit's return to Daytona International Speedway in July for the first race there since Earnhardt Sr.'s death, Junior visited the track with a small group of friends and walked over to the fourth-turn spot where his father had crashed, seeking and finding a kind of closure.

Remarkably, a much more public sealing of that wound occurred a few days later when Junior won that July 7 race, scoring on the track that had claimed his father's life. After he took the checkered flag to officially register one of the most emotional wins in NASCAR history, Junior stopped his race car on the infield grass, jumped from the driver-side door, and began a wild celebration as fans in the main grandstand joined in.

GREEN FLAG

I will instruct you and teach you in the way you should go; I will guide you with My eye.

PSALM 32:8

/// The buildup to Junior's Cup series debut in 1999 was overwhelming. Because he was his father's son, the interest level surrounding Junior was remarkably high, and he went through dozens of interviews before the big day. Asked to compare himself to his father, Junior said, "We're not that much alike. We don't like the same kind of music, and there's a lot of other things, too. I like Pearl Jam, alternative rock, Elvis Presley, seventies soul, and rock music. Dad, he just listens to country. I think he needs to spread out a little more than that."

As the season continued, Junior persevered with grit and determination, just as he knew his father would have wanted. He raced again and won again, and many of the millions of fans who had followed his father moved their allegiance to him. He continues to race in the long shadow of his father's career.

"I know that it'll be many, many years, and if I'm lucky to even come close to the comparison of what my father's done," Junior said. "But each thing I do is a step in that direction to be known as one of those good drivers."

Junior made it through one of the most difficult periods of life to emerge on the other side as a success, even as much of the sports world watched. It took the kind of inner strength that many struggle to find in the wake of losses and trials.

....

FOLLOWING IN A PARENT'S STEPS IS NO EASY TASK,

especially when that parent walks with giants. Innately, children want to please their parents. Sons particularly want their fathers' approval. Even when a father has taken time to instill confidence and encourage his sons through loving guidance and instruction, facing the death of a beloved father and taking up his mantle is an overwhelming task. Such was the case of Solomon, King David's son.

The whirl of a slingshot, then the slap of a stone—direct hit. Then came an earthshaking thud. Goliath, Israel's dreaded loud-mouth enemy, lay dead. Daily, the nine-foot giant had railed Israel's warriors with a barrage of insults. "Why have you come out to line up for battle? Am I not a Philistine, and you the servants of Saul? Choose a man for yourselves, and let him come down to me. If he is able to fight with me and kill me, then we will be your servants. But if I prevail against him and kill him, then you shall be our servants and serve us" (1 Samuel 17:8–9).

David, then just a young shepherd, took the challenge, and now the giant lay helpless at his feet. This was the beginning of David's greatness and the beginning of many victories for Israel under his military leadership. During his forty-year reign as king, David, God's chosen servant, united the kingdom of Israel and ushered in a golden age of peace.

Before King David died, God instructed him to anoint Solomon, his youngest son, as Israel's king. What an awesome responsibility for Solomon! Not only was he to take his father's throne, but he also was to build the grand temple of God. Before David died, he gave Solomon priceless advice: always please God, and God will bless your efforts.

Solomon was humbled after his father's death. How could he walk in the shadow of his father's achievements? Could he be a man, be strong, and follow God? Would he be able to build the magnificent temple?

God knows our hearts, our motives, and our deepest desires, even when we do not fully realize them. One night God appeared to Solomon in a dream and said, "Ask for whatever you want me to give

> The father of the righteous will greatly rejoice,
>
> And he who begets a wise child will delight in him.
>
> **PROVERBS 23:24**

/// Dale Earnhardt Jr. broke into NASCAR major-series success by winning the Coca-Cola 300 Busch series race at Texas Motor Speedway April 4, 1998. Within a few minutes after the victory, Earnhardt Jr.'s souvenir location at the track sold out of every available item.

ALONG THE ROAD

GIANTS OF FAITH ARE PLANTED IN GOD'S WORD AND FILLED WITH HIS WISDOM.

Want to know the best thing to do? Just talk to God. Prayer is that simple. He knows your needs before you ask. But, through prayer, you get to know how good He is.

you" (1 Kings 3:5 NIV). In the dream Solomon revealed his aching heart. He confessed he was only a child who could not govern the vast number of God's people. He asked God for discernment. And because Solomon didn't ask for riches or a long life, God answered his prayers. He gave him a wise and discerning heart—but also blessed him with riches and prosperity.

Solomon built the glorious temple. Kings came from everywhere just to hear his wisdom. He was known as the wisest man of all the earth. Yet, the wisest thing Solomon ever did was to humbly ask God for help. No matter what our difficult circumstance, what insurmountable task sits in front of us, God wants us to seek Him and His ways. Then He will do for us more than we can imagine.

/// Earnhardt Jr. made his Busch series debut June 22, 1996, at Myrtle Beach Speedway on the coast of South Carolina. That spot was chosen because Junior had run a series of weekly-program races at the short track. He ran with the lead group most of the night and finished fourteenth.

Jack Roush

CHAPTER two

A BRUSH WITH DEATH

// For a quarter century, team owner Jack Roush has led as one of the most accomplished figures in NASCAR racing. A businessman and an engineer, Roush has succeeded in several forms of major-league motorsports, and his NASCAR teams have won multiple championships and scored victories in some of the circuit's biggest races.

The biggest miracle in Roush's life, however, had nothing to do with the racetrack.

IN APRIL 2002, Roush, an aviation buff, was flying a small, single-seat plane during an outing near Troy, Alabama. Roush and several of his friends were celebrating his sixtieth birthday, and he had chosen a day of flying as the best way to enjoy the moment.

The day turned dark, however, as Roush maneuvered the small aircraft over the Alabama countryside. He dropped too low and hit a power line, and the plane crashed into a small lake. Suddenly, Roush was unconscious underwater.

He probably would have drowned within minutes, but it so happened that Larry Hicks, an ex-Marine with skills in underwater rescue, had seen the plane fall into the lake near his home. He jumped in his small boat, paddled out to the crash site, and dove into the lake, bravely acting in spite of the gasoline spreading across the water from the plane's damaged fuel tank.

Hicks dove three times before locating the cockpit. He pulled Roush from the seat harness, carried him to the surface, and began performing CPR.

Roush suffered a broken leg, rib fractures, a lung injury, and a closed head injury. Doctors overseeing his care in the days after the crash said fewer than 5 percent of people with similar injuries survive.

"You have to be surrounded by the right people and have the right circumstances for surviving," Roush said. "I certainly had that. I had the chance to fly this little airplane. While doing that, something went really wrong for me. I have no recollection. I can't know if I had trouble with the aircraft or if I had a pilot problem, of judgment. I ran into a wire."

Roush was in rehabilitation for months, but he returned to the racing scene—first on crutches—and now lives a virtually normal life. Since the accident, Roush's teams have won two NASCAR Cup championships and have continued to place among the best on the circuit week-to-week.

Roush quickly acknowledged the heroism of Larry Hicks in saving his life. Hicks traveled to numerous races with the Roush team in the months after the accident and became friends with many of those close to the team.

/// Before launching a successful career in NASCAR racing, Jack Roush was a consistently competitive team owner and car builder in drag racing and sports car racing.

Do not be afraid of sudden terror,
Nor of trouble from the wicked when it comes;
For the LORD will be your confidence,
And will keep your foot from being caught.

PROVERBS 3:25-26

For Roush, the brush with death opened doors on a fuller life.

"EVERY DAY FROM HERE ON OUT IS PRECIOUS BECAUSE THESE ARE EXTRA DAYS," ROUSH SAID.

/// Larry Hicks (left) saved Jack Roush from near-certain death after an airplane accident, and became close to the car owner and his team in the months that followed.

A BRUSH WITH DEATH! It came for all the Jews living in the Persian Empire in the fourth century BC, including Esther and her cousin Mordecai. One of King Xerxes' officials, the deceitful Haman, hated the Jews, especially Mordecai. He planned to annihilate all the Jewish people and hang Mordecai on the gallows. But God intervened, and through the faith and boldness of Esther and Mordecai, the Jews survived.

Xerxes had expelled his wife, Vashti, from the kingdom because she had dared to refuse to parade herself among his drunken guests at his royal banquet. The king's attendants searched for a young virgin to replace her, and he chose the shapely, beautiful Esther, a Jewish orphan raised by her godly cousin Mordecai. But Mordecai warned her

LIFE IS RISKY, DEAR GOD.

I thank You for all the times You have saved me from danger, many times without my knowledge. You are a merciful God, extending our days of life.

Sin pervades our world, and, without Your help, I will fall victim to evil intent. I know You are in control of the world. You search to see if any of us look to You and seek Your face. Fill my life with joy, not fear or pain. Help me make You proud and cherish each day You give. Lord, I trust my life and loved ones in Your care.

////

not to reveal her nationality or family background to the king.

The wicked Haman, a noble of the king's court, despised Mordecai because he refused to bow to him. So when he learned that Mordecai was Jewish, he planned not only to kill him, but also to kill all the Jews in the province. He convinced the king to sign a royal edict to destroy them.

The Jewish people were devastated when they heard the news. Wailing was heard throughout the province, and Mordecai sat in sackcloth and cried in the public streets. When Esther sent her servant to check on him, he sent her a copy of the king's edict and told her to go before the king and beg for mercy for her people. But she knew the royal law—anyone who approached the king without being invited would be put to death.

Brave Esther asked Mordecai to gather all the Jews to fast and pray for her. She said, "When this is done, I will go to the king, even though it is against the law. And if I perish, I perish" (Esther 4:16 NIV).

Mordecai told Esther, "Who knows whether you have come to the kingdom for such a time as this?" (Esther 4:14). God was watching and listening. Empowered by prayer, Esther approached the king. He

CAUTION FLAG

Absolutely no one knows our future but God. Why don't we let Him steer our course?

/// Roush won the NASCAR Cup championship for the first time in 2003 with driver Matt Kenseth.

/// In 2007, Roush sold half of his NASCAR team to Fenway Sports Group, which also owns the Boston Red Sox Major League Baseball team, forming a unique partnership across two sports.

God is ever alert to the changes in the road and will outsmart the curves.

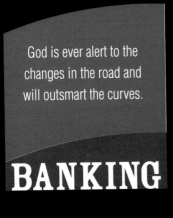

BANKING

/// Roush was inducted into the International Motorsports Hall of Fame in 2006.

was delighted to see her and asked for her request. She asked that he and Haman come to a banquet she had prepared. Pleased, the king relayed the message to Haman.

Haman was ecstatic about his special invitation and eagerly came to dine with the king and Esther. But to his horrified surprise, at the feast Esther revealed Haman's plan to destroy her people. The king, enraged, hanged Haman on the very gallows Haman had built for Mordecai. The Jews were saved, and Mordecai and Esther were greatly revered.

God is always in control of the events in our lives—our brushes with death are not coincidental. Precious lives are saved when God's people pray and spiritual giants stand up to the enemy. Will we obey when God asks us to take a risk of faith? With His help, we can rise to the challenge.

ALONG THE ROAD

GOD DOESN'T NEED A WATCH. HE CONTROLS TIME.

Nothing we do hurries God. He's always punctual, never late. We can trust His timing and wisdom in all of our circumstances.

/// Roush started his NASCAR career with Arkansas native Mark Martin driving for his team. Martin finished second in the Cup championship standings four times while driving for Roush.

All the days ordained for me were written in your book before one of them came to be.

PSALM 139:16 NIV

Carl Edwards

CHAPTER three

CREATIVITY

PAYS OFF

// There is no question that racing at NASCAR's top level is one of the most difficult jobs in the sporting world. What's harder? Getting to the top level.

All across the United States—and even across its borders north and south—thousands of race car drivers see NASCAR's Cup circuit as the ultimate goal. They race virtually every week, sometimes several days a week, at backwoods dirt short tracks, honing their skills, building their resumés, and hoping for a shot at the big time.

FOR MOST, THAT CHANCE NEVER COMES. Even if they're talented, they never make the right connection to get to the top. NASCAR Cup fields have room for only forty-three drivers. When a team has a vacancy, literally thousands of hopefuls might long for it.

So how does a successful short-track driver make it to the big show? Often, it's all about connections. Or relatives—a driver's uncle knows a team owner, for example. Or a car owner looking for a new, young driver just happens to be at the right track at the right time when a newcomer shines, and the foundation for a deal is made.

One of the latest "he came from nowhere" stories belongs to Carl Edwards, a Missouri resident who drives for Roush Fenway Racing and has become a weekly victory threat in NASCAR racing.

The son of a short-track racer, Edwards grew up at the racetrack and was driving a go-kart by the age of four. He was good from the start, and by the age of thirteen he had moved into small mini-sprint cars. After several years of success on short tracks—and with his mother, Nancy, having invested most of the family's savings in his race car—Edwards was still looking for his break into the big time.

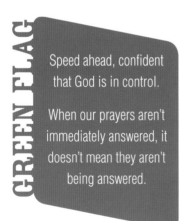

GREEN FLAG

Speed ahead, confident that God is in control.

When our prayers aren't immediately answered, it doesn't mean they aren't being answered.

Then he had an unusual idea. He decided to separate himself from other would-be stars by using a business card. At a cost of $130, he printed 3,000 cards with his name, resumé, and contact information, along with the phrase, "If you're looking for a driver, you're looking for me." He started handing them out to anyone who would stop and listen. He also placed copies of the card in the classified sections of racing magazines.

"My mission was to let potential owners know that I wanted to drive race cars," Edwards said. "It was kind of awkward to just walk up to people and tell them, 'Hey, I want to drive your car.' So I thought having a business card would kind of make it a little more natural. I had a lot of people make fun of me, but it worked out."

Edwards landed a part-time ride with team owner Mike Mittler in NASCAR's Craftsman Truck Series, and impressive drives there gained him the notice of Cup team owner Jack Roush. In 2003, Roush invited Edwards to join his operation, and he quickly accepted.

Edwards has raced to a championship in NASCAR's No. 2 series, has scored several Cup victories, and has challenged for the Cup championship. He is expected to be a major NASCAR star for many years to come.

THANKS, IN PART, TO HIS INNOVATIVE BUSINESS CARD.

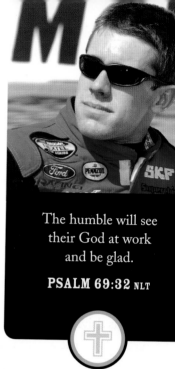

The humble will see their God at work and be glad.

PSALM 69:32 NLT

/// Edwards has a fledgling sideline business. He owns Back40 Records, a recording studio in his hometown of Columbia, Missouri.

/// Edwards frequently gives his race-winning trophies to children or other special guests at racetracks.

/// Edwards finished tenth in his NASCAR Cup Series debut in August 2004 in Brooklyn, Michigan. Only a handful of drivers have scored top-ten finishes in their initial races.

GOD BLESSED THE ISRAELITES and multiplied them while they were living in Egypt. But as their numbers grew, the pharaoh felt threatened, so he enslaved them. Day after day, God's people cried out to Him because of their cruel taskmasters. It seemed their prayers would not be heard.

Meanwhile, Pharaoh showed no mercy. He even commanded the Egyptians to throw every Israelite boy that was born into the Nile River.

But God spared the baby Moses by giving his mother an innovative idea. Moses' mother laid him in a tar-pitched basket made of papyrus reeds and laid it near the edge of the Nile where the princess of Egypt bathed. When the princess heard the baby's cries, she had compassion on him and adopted him as her own. As planned, Miriam, Moses' sister, asked the princess if she could find a Hebrew nursemaid for the child, and brought her own mother to nurse Moses.

Moses grew up in Pharaoh's court, but he felt compassion for his own people. While visiting the Israelites one day, he saw an Egyptian beating a Hebrew—and he killed the Egyptian. When he realized the deed had become known, he had to escape to Midian because Pharaoh sought to kill him.

There in the desert Moses experienced God's call on his life, even if he didn't see it coming. As a young man in Pharaoh's court, he had learned the ways of the Egyptians. Now, as a shepherd for his father-in-law in Midian, he came to know the desert—the same desert where he would eventually lead the people of Israel for forty years. In that wilderness, he had time to reflect on his parents' great faith, God's mercy to him, and the oppression of the Hebrew people. What he didn't realize was that these years were preparation for a great task ahead.

Be patient and prepare for the long road ahead. Worrying will only slow you down.

PIT STOP

/// Prior to becoming a full-time racer, Edwards was a substitute teacher in his hometown.

O YE OF LITTLE FAITH

Do we think God asleep
when He does not keep

In time with our cries
and cares?

Would we show ill will
and hurt Him still

With our whimpers, sighs,
and groans?

Let us trust His grace
and seek His face

For he shushes every moan.

Working behind the scenes
such miraculous schemes,

He performs His holy will.

With hand-held brushes,
adding gentle touches,

He answers His
children's prayers.

POLLY HEMBREE

/ Carl Edwards has a unique way of celebrating
s victories. He stands on the door panel of his
ace car and backflips into the air and onto the
round, a trick he learned from a gymnast friend.

When Moses was eighty years old, God called to him from a burning bush near Mount Sinai. Out of the flames, God spoke to Moses concerning His compassion toward Israel. He had heard their cries of suffering: "I know their sorrows. So I have come down to deliver them out of the hand of the Egyptians, and to bring them up from that land to a good and large land, to a land flowing with milk and honey" (Exodus 3:7–8).

When God told Moses He was sending him to rescue Israel, he was shocked. "Who am I that I should go to Pharaoh?" he asked (Exodus 3:11). God assured him He would be with him—and He even provided him with an amazing staff that would serve as his credentials. When Moses threw it on the ground in front of Pharaoh's officials, it became a hissing snake.

God had poised Moses to be the answer to his people's prayers. By faith, he performed many God-signs in Egypt. By God's hand, disastrous plagues sent Egypt reeling. And miraculously, Moses led Israel out of Egypt. At God's command, Moses stretched forth this staff, and the Red Sea divided for the Israelites to walk through on dry land, then closed and drowned the pursuing Egyptians. The Israelites walked to freedom.

The pitched basket, the flaming bush, the changing staff, diverse plagues, and a parted sea—all of these were creative ways God used to deliver His people. When it seems that God has turned a deaf ear to our prayers, we must recall His mighty works. He is an inventive God who is always at work bringing about His divine plan and purpose in our lives. We need only to trust Him.

 DEAR LORD, how great are Your works! Thank You for Your tender mercies to us. Forgive our doubts and help us to trust in You always, for You are an awesome God.

Why do you say, O Jacob,

And speak, O Israel:

"My way is hidden from the LORD,

And my just claim is passed over by my God"?

Have you not known?

Have you not heard?

The everlasting God, the LORD, . . .

Neither faints nor is weary. . . .

He gives power to the weak,

And to those who have no might

He increases strength.

ISAIAH 40:27-29

Dale Earnhardt Sr.

CHAPTER four

SMALL BEGINNINGS LEAD TO GREAT THINGS

// In almost every sport, rookies usually find the going tough. That can be especially true in NASCAR, where every speedway is different, circumstances change wildly from race to race, and veteran drivers tend to be wary of newcomers.

Additionally, NASCAR Cup races are much longer than those normally experienced by drivers in the early years of their careers. Races are typically 400 to 500 miles on the circuit's longer tracks and 500 laps on half-mile courses.

In the long race of life, we can be fueled with the living water of God's Spirit when we know the dynamics of Christ's love.

PIT STOP

/// In 1994, Earnhardt Sr. pulled alongside one of the sport's other giants, Richard Petty, in a key statistical column. Earnhardt won his seventh Cup champion-ship, tying Petty for the all-time lead in that category.

THE CUP SERIES' LONGEST RACE IS THE COCA-COLA 600, which is run each May at Lowe's Motor Speedway near Charlotte, North Carolina. The marathon typically takes four and a half to five hours to complete, and, particularly if the weather is warm, drivers are unusually weary when the long day is finally over.

Oddly, seven-time Cup champion Dale Earnhardt Sr., one of the greatest drivers in the history of the sport, picked the 600 to make his Cup debut. He raced in NASCAR's top series for the first time on May 25, 1975.

DEAR LORD, redirect our steps to the ones who need You most. We are the church, Your body, Your presence in the world. Empower our witness and broaden our vision. The day is short; the night far spent. Yet in test and trial, You have blessed us still and filled our cups with love and everlasting life. Send us to labor for You, Lord.

Earnhardt had had success on short tracks in his native North Carolina, but, mostly because of financial reasons, he hadn't been able to break into the major leagues of stock car racing. That changed because of his friendship with Norman Negre, the son of veteran Cup driver Ed Negre.

Norman Negre worked on Earnhardt's cars as the young driver moved from track to track in the Carolinas, scoring wins and strong finishes. Negre, impressed with Earnhardt's skill and determination, was convinced that he had a bright future.

Whatever the track, whatever the challenge, go in Christ's name.

GO THE IIII DISTANCE

So Negre talked to his father, the owner of a very small Cup operation. As a result of that conversation, Ed Negre, who also was a driver, entered a second car in the 600 for Earnhardt. Negre agreed to give Earnhardt a shot if he and Norman Negre would prepare the car.

They jumped at the chance. Negre let them use a 1975 Dodge Charger, and Earnhardt qualified for the race. There was no rush of publicity or grand entrance for Earnhardt, a virtual unknown in those days despite the fact that his father, Ralph, had been a successful NASCAR short-track racer.

He started the race in thirty-third position and finished twenty-second, winning only $2,425. At that point in life, he was satisfied simply to finish a race so dramatically longer than any he had previously attempted.

In fact, the length of the race resulted in an unscheduled pit stop for Earnhardt.

"I asked Norman what was wrong," Ed Negre said of Earnhardt's stop. "He said, 'There's nothing wrong.' He laughed and said Dale stopped for a drink of water. He'd never run a 600-mile race. He was one worn-out kid when that race was over."

Richard Petty won the race, with Earnhardt forty-five laps behind at the finish. Not a splendid start, but it gave Earnhardt an opening. And five years later, he had the first of his seven championships.

IT WAS A TOUGH INITIATION, BUT THE ULTIMATE REWARDS WERE PLENTIFUL.

> "I am the bread of life. He who comes to Me shall never hunger, and he who believes in Me shall never thirst."
>
> **JOHN 6:35**

/// Earnhardt Sr. scored his final Cup victory October 15, 2000, at Talladega Superspeedway in Alabama in one of the most dramatic races in series history. Earnhardt roared from eighteenth place with five laps to go to take the win.

THE WOMAN OF SAMARIA WAS NOBODY. Her name is unknown, yet her faith and fearless testimony of Jesus brought a whole town out to meet Him.

On His way to Galilee from Judea, tired and thirsty, Jesus made an unscheduled stop in Samaria at Jacob's well. There He met a Samaritan woman who came to draw water. She came at noon when no one else would be present, perhaps to avoid the other women's stark rejection and cruel stares, for she lived an immoral life.

Jesus asked her for a drink of water, taking her completely by surprise. After all, the Jews had nothing to do with Samaritans, and men rarely spoke to strange women, especially her kind. Curious, she spoke her mind, asking why He would ask her for water. He responded, "If you knew the gift of God, and who it is who says to you, 'Give Me a drink,' you would have asked Him, and He would have given you living water" (John 4:10). He told her that the water He would give her would become a perpetual spring of everlasting life within her, and she would never thirst again.

Misunderstanding, she asked Jesus for the water to drink so she wouldn't have to trudge to the well each day—a respite from all the

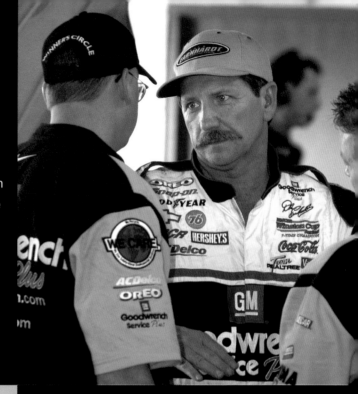

/// Dale Earnhardt Sr. earned his first NASCAR Cup victory at one of the series' toughest tracks—Bristol Motor Speedway in the mountains of east Tennessee. Earnhardt won there April 1, 1979, on the way to taking the series' rookie of the year title that season.

WE ARE ALL
CHAMPIONS
WHEN WE PUT
CHRIST FIRST IN
ALL WE DO.

mockery she experienced daily. Knowing her heart, He asked her to go back home and bring her husband. "I have no husband," she replied (John 4:17). Jesus then exposed her sins. He told her the harsh truth: she had had five husbands, and the man she was living with was not her husband.

Uncomfortable, she quickly changed the subject to talk about where one should worship. The Jews insisted that Jerusalem was the only place to worship, she told Him, but the Samaritans believed it was on Mount Gerizin. Jesus explained that the place of worship is not important, but it is important

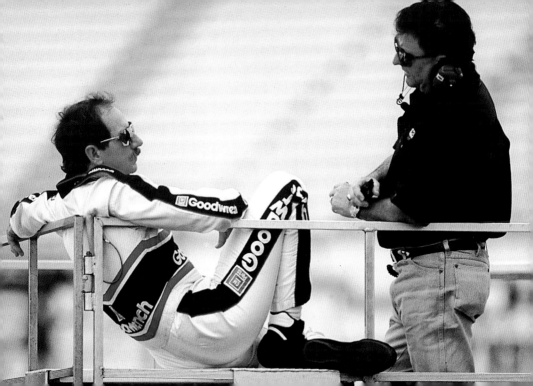

"I have come that they might have life, and that they may have it more abundantly."

JOHN 10:10

CHAPTER five

RISING

TO THE CHALLENGE

Juan Pablo Montoya

// Juan Pablo Montoya, a native of Colombia, joined the NASCAR Cup Series in 2007, bringing along quite a resumé.

Montoya, who was raised on road-course racing, had built an international reputation racing in Indianapolis-style cars and on the worldwide Formula One circuit, where he stormed capitals on several continents and won races against some of the world's best drivers.

MONTOYA, NOW A RESIDENT OF MIAMI, FLORIDA, took a startling turn in his career in 2007, however, deciding to give NASCAR a try and teaming with his former boss, car owner Chip Ganassi.

Although Montoya had raced on oval tracks, which make up the vast majority of NASCAR venues, he'd spent most of his career on road courses, and he had never driven the much heavier, less responsive stock cars used in NASCAR's top series. Additionally, Montoya had never even seen—much less raced on—most NASCAR tracks.

Clearly, he faced a steep learning curve. And nowhere was that climb expected to be tougher than at legendary Darlington Raceway in Darlington, South Carolina.

LORD, too many times I fail to pray and seek Your will, so I make a lot of mistakes. I want to be a good parent and a good Christian, but I need Your help. When I meet new challenges and I'm uncertain of the decisions I should make, remind me of Your love and of the humble Joseph, who trusted and followed You.

Opened in 1950, Darlington Raceway is the oldest large track on the NASCAR circuit. Narrow passing lanes and difficult turns—all in an oblong shape that makes one end tighter than the other—make up the 1.3 miles in this formidable course.

With God, there is always a better alternative.
||||BALANCE

Even some of NASCAR's veteran drivers haven't figured out how to drive Darlington properly, and some drivers who won easily at other tracks never wrote their names on Darlington's list of champions. Winning there is considered a strong endorsement of a driver's skill, patience, and smarts.

So Montoya, all new to this game, approached the Dodge Avenger 500 at the old track on May 13, 2007, as a considerable challenge. In opening-round practice the day before the scheduled race, he got his first taste of what lay ahead of him.

/// Juan Pablo Montoya has scored victories at some of racing's most historic sites, including Indianapolis Motor Speedway, where he won the Indianapolis 500 in 2000, and Monaco, where he won one of Formula One's classic races in 2003.

/// Montoya supports the children of his native Colombia through the Montoya family's Formula Smiles Foundation, which funds recreational facilities in the South American country.

Life doesn't always run smoothly. With God's promises we can rise above our problems and make wise decisions.

//// BALANCE

"The tires don't even feel good when they're brand-new," Montoya said. "It's hard in your mind when there's no grip out there. The way you have to get on the gas is more like a road course. It's hard to know how deep to go into turn two to cut the corner. You go too deep, you get out of the gas and you miss the corner and hit the wall. You go too early, you run wide and you hit the wall. There has to be a happy medium."

Finding that medium is the trick at Darlington, and that's a task that most first-time drivers don't accomplish. Simply completing the entire distance in the first race on such a tough track is generally considered a significant achievement.

Halfway through the long day, Montoya was twenty-eighth. A few laps later, he and fellow rookie A. J. Allmendinger were wrestling for position, and the front end of Montoya's car tapped Allmendinger's. The damage affected the performance of Montoya's car the rest of the way.

Montoya finished twenty-third—not exactly what he wanted, but nevertheless a good day for a newcomer at Darlington. He had avoided calamity and learned a lot on a day when tests came at him hard and heavy.

LIFE CONTINUALLY PRESENTS US WITH DIFFICULT CHALLENGES.

The most complex are those in which uncertainty strangles our decision-making process. No matter which turn we take, without divine intervention, calamity seems to be ahead of us. Joseph, the husband of Mary, faced such hard decisions.

> For everyone who asks receives, and he who seeks finds, and to him who knocks it will be opened.
>
> **MATTHEW 7:8**

Joseph was a devout Jew, a descendant of King David. He was engaged to Mary, a humble servant of God, and would soon bring her home as his wife. He loved and trusted Mary, but his promised one had become pregnant. It seemed impossible! He thought about divorcing her quietly.

But God changed his plans one fateful night. Weary, Joseph fell asleep. As he slept, an angel spoke to him in a dream: "Do not be afraid to take Mary home as your wife, because what is conceived in her is from the Holy Spirit. She will give birth to a son, and you are to give him the name Jesus, because he will save his people from their sins" (Matthew 1:20–21 NIV). Joseph awoke. He knew God was speaking to him. Believing and trusting God, he took Mary as his wife, but did not have relations with her until after the child was born.

Just before the baby's birth, in a turn of events that slightly upgraded the challenges faced by this small family, the governor required Joseph to register for a census in his hometown of Bethlehem. It would be a difficult trip, especially with Mary so far into her pregnancy. When they arrived, Mary began having labor pains, but Joseph couldn't find a vacant room. Finally, he found a cattle

Traveling at high speeds and making split-second decisions is dangerous. Trying to "wing it" without God can be just as costly.

IIIIBALANCE

Stop!

There is impending danger. Don't try to handle the problem by yourself. Seek spiritual guidance.

stall, and there Mary gave birth to her son. When the tiny babe came, Mary could relax and gaze on God's Son. It was a holy moment for all of them—and for all of us. Joseph named the baby Jesus, as the angel had said.

In the late hours of the night, a strange thing happened. A group of tattered shepherds came and bowed before the child. A choir of angels had appeared to them in the dark sky, singing and praising God. Jesus, the angels said, was to bring peace to the world.

About two years later, wise men from the East followed a bright star to Bethlehem. They, too, bowed before Jesus, bringing him rich gifts. Joseph and Mary stood in awe of God's works.

God would continue to guide the trio closely. Soon an angel came to Joseph again, warning him that Herod planned to kill the baby and instructing him to take Jesus to Egypt. New challenges lay ahead—traveling to a foreign county secretly, finding and succeeding at a new job, caring for his wife and Jesus. But we can only guess that God provided for Joseph, Mary, and Jesus the way He had been doing all along. The family settled in Egypt, and there they lived until the angel appeared and directed Joseph to take the family to Nazareth.

Joseph is a giant father-figure. God entrusted His Son to his care. He faced challenging decisions as a husband and father, but he looked to God for direction. When the road of life was uncertain for Joseph, he turned to God, and so can we. God delights to make His will known to us.

For I know the thoughts that I think toward you, says the
LORD, thoughts of peace and not of evil, to give you a future
and a hope. Then you will call upon Me and go and pray to Me,
and I will listen to you. And you will seek Me and find Me,

CHAPTER SIX

BLESSINGS
IN DISGUISE

// As early as his preteen years, Kyle Busch had his eye on NASCAR Cup racing.

The younger brother (by seven years) of established NASCAR star Kurt Busch, Kyle followed directly in his sibling's tire tracks, succeeding in go-kart racing and moving on to short-track stock car racing. The brothers raced against each other repeatedly, and despite the difference in age, Kyle always considered himself a threat to outrun Kurt.

Slow down.

God may be leading you in a new direction. Be sensitive to His call.

WITH THE ASSISTANCE OF THEIR FATHER, Tom, both brothers made quick advances as they moved through ever-tougher levels of motorsports. Kyle benefited from the trails his brother blazed, and it became evident to observers even in his teenage years that he was destined to have a shot at stardom in a major racing series.

That chance came very quickly. After success on short tracks near the Busch family's home in Las Vegas, Nevada, Kyle moved into a ride in NASCAR's Craftsman Truck Series at the almost-ready-to-shave age of sixteen. Despite the pressure of performing against older, more experienced drivers and racing on faster tracks, he did well, and he and those involved in his career were clearly positioning him to move into Cup racing as soon as possible—almost certainly before his eighteenth birthday.

Then, suddenly, that door slammed. NASCAR changed its rules, deciding that drivers younger than eighteen could not race in any of its top three series, then called the Nextel Cup Series, Busch Series, and Craftsman Truck Series.

Busch was devastated. It was as if someone pulled the rug from under his feet as he ran at full speed. He suddenly had nowhere to go.

Although he had established himself at higher levels of competition, he joined the short-track American Speed Association Late Model series in 2002 and raced out of the spotlight. It was a tough pill to swallow for a young man on the move, but he needed to continue racing and sharpen his skills.

/// A swift and early learner, Kyle Busch started in six NASCAR Craftsman Truck Series races in 2001 when he was still a high school junior (and before NASCAR changed its age rules). He finished in the top ten in two of those events.

A man's heart plans his way,

But the LORD directs his steps.

PROVERBS 16:9

Recuperate.
Find some quiet time to pray. Listen and be ready for changes.

OFF SEASON

"I felt like the whole world was taken from me and what I wanted I couldn't have anymore," Busch said. "For me, being that young, I thought, 'I'm done, there's no more of me.' You're there and you get kicked out and you think, 'Well, who's going to want me now?'"

In hindsight, though, the big switch was good for Busch. It gave him time for more seasoning before he tackled faster and better traffic at NASCAR's top levels, and it proved to him that sometimes waiting is better.

"Going to ASA and learning the things I was able to learn there about longer races, pit stops, strategy, this and that was really, really good for me instead of just driving the race car and have the crew chief make all the calls," Busch said. "I kind of have a sense of what I need to know about a race and how it plays out. Now if I was in the Cup series at eighteen, I would be lost. Completely lost."

Busch eventually moved into Busch and Cup racing and, in his early twenties, is one of the best drivers in the sport.

HIS DETOUR—HOWEVER FRUSTRATING AT THE MOMENT—WAS A BLESSING IN DISGUISE.

LORD, have mercy on me, for I am a sinner. All my life I have gone my own way. Now show me Your way. Thank You, Jesus, for dying for me. Forgive my sin and give me the joy of the Ethiopian, who gave his life to You.

WE MAY INITIALLY QUESTION OUR DETOURS, but they can turn out to be blessings, not only for us, but also for others. This was the case with Philip, the evangelist in the book of Acts.

Philip, along with other deacons, helped distribute food to the widows in the early church in Jerusalem. Grave persecution, however, forced Philip and other Christians to flee to other areas. Obeying the words of Christ to "go therefore and make disciples of all the nations" (Matthew 28:19), Philip went to Samaria, a place where none of the disciples had gone, perhaps because of Jewish prejudice toward the Samaritans. Philip preached boldly, and many Samaritans became Christians.

While Philip was in Samaria, an angel of the Lord spoke to him: "Go south to the road—the desert road—that goes down from Jerusalem to Gaza" (Acts 8:26 NIV). Philip obeyed. Along the way he saw an influential Ethiopian who was in charge of the queen's treasury. The man was on his way home from worship in Jerusalem. When Philip heard him reading from Isaiah about the suffering servant, he knew why the angel had directed him to go south. The Spirit of God told him to go to the chariot and stay near it.

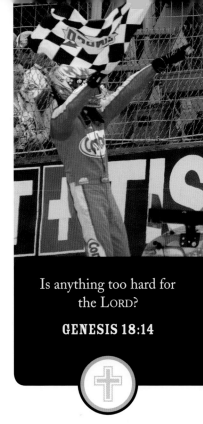

Is anything too hard for the LORD?

GENESIS 18:14

/// In 2005, Busch won two races in his Cup rookie season, becoming one of only a handful of drivers to win multiple races as a first-year driver.

Philip asked the man if he understood what he was reading. The man then asked Philip to sit in the chariot and explain the passage to him. Philip explained that the slaughtered lamb the book of Isaiah referred to was none other than Jesus Christ.

He went on to explain the message of Christ that millions have come to know today. God gave His Son Jesus to die for our sins. Three days later, He raised Him from the dead. Afterward, Jesus appeared to many in Jerusalem and then went back to heaven and sat at the right hand of the Father. Anyone who in prayer confesses his sins and asks Jesus to become his Lord will be given eternal life and will become a child of God. Because the Ethiopian believed the truth of Christ with all his heart, he went home a happy new person.

Whatever our present situation and regardless of our past mistakes, Jesus can fill the void in our lives and give us the joy this Ethiopian and many others have experienced. We may have to make a detour from the road we are now traveling, but a new life and direction await us as we take a giant step of faith.

ALONG THE ROAD

WE ARE NEVER SURE WHERE GOD WILL LEAD US, BUT WE ARE CONFIDENT IT WILL BE IN THE RIGHT DIRECTION.

Obedience to God's ways opens up new doors and blessings.

THE ROAD OF LIFE HAS MANY DETOURS, BUT GOD IS THERE TOO.

POEM OF PRAISE

Praise the Lord for His love.

Praise Him for His care.

Thank Him for His amazing grace

That finds us anywhere.

When we race off—go our own way,

He redirects our route,

Forgives our sin, and fills our lives

With love to spread about.

POLLY HEMBREE

CHAPTER seven

BIG SHOES
TO FILL

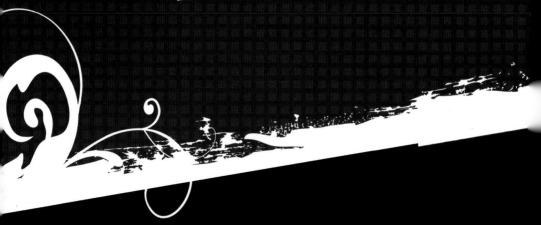

JEFF GORDON

// **Jeff Gordon** entered NASCAR Cup racing in 1992 having built a strong resumé in Midwest sprint and midget-car racing. Team owner Rick Hendrick saw the promise in Gordon during a second-level NASCAR race at Atlanta Motor Speedway and offered him a contract to go Cup racing.

Thus began one of the most remarkable success stories in the history of the sport. Gordon has won races and championships with admirable regularity and is universally recognized as one of the greatest drivers in the wide sweep of NASCAR racing. In addition, with his good looks and media-savvy approach to his job, he has transformed the way many people see the sport and brought new fans into the mix.

POLE //// POSITION

You are in the prime spot. Be thankful for all those who helped put you there and expect expert competition.

/// Gordon has won more than $100 million in his racing career, easily the top total in NASCAR history.

DESPITE HIS TALENTS, HOWEVER,

Gordon didn't find an easy road. A few people stood in the way of his success—notably the Intimidator himself, Dale Earnhardt Sr. Earnhardt ruled the sport in the early 1990s. He won four of his record seven championships in the five-year stretch from 1990 to 1994. During that period, he won an astonishing twenty-four races.

Into the arena stepped Gordon, and soon he was seen as the young, up-and-coming challenger to Earnhardt's status. In fact, Gordon won his first Cup championship in 1995, ending a two-year run by Earnhardt, and he followed with championships in 1997 and 1998.

DEAR FATHER, You desire mercy and obedience. Help me to show others mercy as You have shown me. Let me not compare myself to others but be confident in the gifts You have given me. Help me obey Your Word and trust Your guidance. I am a sinner and know I fail You many times, but please forgive my pride and self-absorption. May I always remember my mission in life is to honor You and turn my whole heart to You.

Still, Gordon continued to face the Earnhardt questions. Which driver was the better of the two, and could Gordon challenge Earnhardt's records? Was Gordon's finesse style of driving better than Earnhardt's rough-and-ready approach? And how would they race each other on the track as they wrestled for the same high ground?

"My first real valuable lesson was in 1993 when I was a rookie," Gordon said. "We were racing at Phoenix. He was a little better than I was. I was running ninth or tenth. He got underneath me, and I

The race of life brings bumps, spins, and winding curves. Remain faithful to your charge. God is with you.

||||||HANDLING THE PRESSURE

raced him really hard. We went into (turn) three and— boom!—I was in the wall. I remember that being a valuable lesson to me. I think that was a way for him to teach the rookie how things were going to be."

Earnhardt would test the young driver again and again. "I think Jeff knew he had to earn Earnhardt's respect," said Terry Labonte, a Gordon teammate and a longtime Earnhardt friend. "I think there for a while he didn't realize he was going to have to earn it every week. He made that comment to me one time."

In 2007, Gordon surpassed Earnhardt's career win total of seventy-six, restarting comparisons between the two even after Earnhardt's death.

IN THE END, GORDON LEARNED HIS LESSONS WELL.

DAVID, JUST A YOUNG SHEPHERD

at the time, became mighty King Saul's greatest challenge. On David's return from one of Israel's battles, the women from all the towns began celebrating, playing tambourines and cymbals and singing: "Saul has killed his thousands, and David his ten thousands" (1 Samuel 18:7 NLT). Their praise of David angered Saul. He sensed that David could be the king who would replace him.

Years earlier, Samuel, the prophet of God, had anointed Saul as the first king of Israel. He was handsome and daring, a man head-and-shoulders taller than the other Israelites. God's Spirit came upon Saul and gave him great military success. The people responded with gratitude and love for their new king.

/// Jeff Gordon made his Cup series debut in the final race of the 1992 season at Atlanta Motor Speedway. The race marked the intertwining of two eras as longtime NASCAR star Richard Petty raced for the final time.

> Some trust in chariots and some in horses, but we trust in the name of the LORD our God.
>
> **PSALM 20:7** NIV

Saul, however, began to take credit for God's work. He became rebellious and disobedient to God. In Carmel he set up a monument to honor himself after victory against the Amalekites. God had instructed him through the prophet Samuel to destroy all the Amalekites and their possessions, but he brought back King Agag with him and the country's choicest sheep and cattle. Saul's excuse for his disobedience was that he intended to offer the animals as sacrifices to God. But Samuel admonished him, "to obey is better than sacrifice" (1 Samuel 15:22). Because Saul had rejected God's command, God rejected him as king. His kingdom would be given to one better than he, one who would seek God with his whole heart.

Unknown to Saul, God had instructed Samuel to anoint David as the next king when David was a young shepherd. David trusted in God with his whole heart and wrote songs of praise to Him. God kept him safe from wild animals while he was taking care of his sheep in the mountains, empowered him to kill the giant Goliath, and gave him great victory as Saul's general.

Realizing God's Spirit had left him, Saul sometimes acted like a raving madman. David would play his harp to help soothe his troubled mind, but Saul began to understand that God's blessings had left him and now rested on David. He knew God would give his kingdom to David, not to one of his sons. During one of David's songs, Saul slung his spear in rage at David to kill him, but God protected him.

David immediately left the palace—and became a fugitive because of Saul's jealousy toward him. As Saul continued his hunt for David, several opportunities arose for David to kill the king, but he refused to lay a hand on God's anointed one. After many battles, the Philistines finally killed King Saul and three of his sons at Mount Gilboa. David grieved for King Saul and his sons and even composed a funeral song for Saul and his son Jonathan. Many years later, David became the anointed king of Israel.

Pride and disobedience were Saul's demise. These sins not only affected him but also his family—his sons died and did not inherit the throne. God chose David—not a perfect young man, but one who wanted to please God, one who prayed and honored Him—to take up Saul's mantle. God's Spirit blessed David. We, too, can know God's blessings as we seek to follow Him with our whole hearts.

ALONG THE ROAD

WHEN WE COMPARE OURSELVES TO OTHERS, WE FORGET THE UNIQUENESS GOD HAS GIVEN US.

We race to win the prize, looking to Christ the author and finisher of our faith.

Do you not know that those who

run in a race all run, but one receives

the prize? Run in such a way that

you may obtain it. And everyone who

competes for the prize is temperate

in all things. Now they do it to obtain

a perishable crown, but we for an

imperishable crown.

1 CORINTHIANS 9:24-25

CHAPTER eight

CHARACTER
UNDER PRESSURE

Mark Martin

// As long as there is stock car racing, Mark Martin will be remembered as one of the sport's great drivers.

Martin, a longtime traveler of NASCAR roads who started his major-league racing career in 1981, is a racer's racer. Hard-nosed but fair, extremely talented, steadfast, and patient, Martin has won the respect of virtually everyone he has raced against.

It is honorable for a man
to stop striving,

Since any fool can start
a quarrel.

PROVERBS 20:3

/// Considered an elite
driver by his contempo-
raries, Martin has been a
dependable winner and
top-ten driver through
much of his career. For
twelve straight seasons,
from 1989 to 2000, he
finished in the top ten
in Cup points.

ALTHOUGH HE HAS WON REPEATEDLY

and is a certain Hall of Fame choice, Martin
has fallen short in two areas that carry much
weight in NASCAR racing: he has never
won a Cup championship (he has finished
fourth twice), and he has never won the
Daytona 500, NASCAR's most important
and richest race.

So, despite decades of success, Martin
has endured his share of heartbreaking disappointment. That experience was no more
vivid than in the final moments of the 2007
Daytona 500, a race in which Martin almost
ended more than two decades of frustration
trying to win NASCAR's marquee event.

Almost.

The race, the forty-ninth Daytona 500,
started slowly, with much single-file racing,
but the final fifty laps were jammed with action, crashes, and drama at the front.

The decision came down to Kevin
Harvick and Martin. As they ran toward the
finish line on the last lap, Harvick surged
forward to place his car beside Martin's in
the third turn, and they headed for home.

Behind them, as the crowded group at
the front rolled into and out of the final
turn, chaos erupted. Several cars slammed

DEAR LORD, thank You for total, unequivocal forgiveness, for Your life-giving sacrifice to present me without blemish before the Father. Thank You for not remembering—You know my sins. It shames me to mention them. Give me a kind, gracious heart when others hurt me. I don't have that kind of love within myself. Create in me a forgiving heart. Amen.

together, and then others darted high and low in attempts to miss the accident.

Harvick and Martin had not reached the finish line when the wrecking started, and that circumstance created the day's big controversy. NASCAR's rules include the stipulation that the field will be "frozen" (preventing cars from legally passing) if a caution flag is displayed. Martin clearly held a slight lead over Harvick when the crashing started behind them and, by some

God will give us smooth driving, even through the hot spots, when we rely on His Spirit of self-restraint.

////HANDLING

And when you stand praying, if you have anything against anyone, forgive him, that your Father in heaven may also forgive you your trespasses.

MARK 11:25

/// Martin was a success in short-track racing before he moved to NASCAR Cup competition in 1981. His first attempt at big-league racing failed, but he returned with team owner Jack Roush in 1988 and soon began showing the talent that would earn him dozens of wins.

interpretations, should have been awarded the race victory. But NASCAR allowed the two drivers to continue to race full speed to the finish line, and Harvick edged Martin by two one-hundredths of a second.

It was one of the closest finishes in NASCAR history, and Martin again had missed grabbing what would have been the biggest win of his career.

Because of the race's confusing end and, as many observers viewed it, Martin's apparent victory, some assumed the veteran driver would be uncontrollably upset. There he stood on the brink of one of the biggest moments of his career, and he saw it wiped out by a controversial ruling.

Martin, though, showed the class he has displayed so often as he has visited peaks and valleys in his long career. He refused to turn the aftermath of NASCAR's biggest race into a free-for-all argument.

"I have no idea what happened behind me," Martin said. "I know I was ahead when they were wrecking behind me, but my focus was on beating the 29 (Harvick). The reason you're not going to see me argue is that nobody wants to hear a grown man cry. That's what it is, and I'm not going to cry about it."

WE SHOW OUR TRUE CHARACTER when we face disappointment or harsh injustice. To walk away and not seek revenge or harbor malice shows incredible, God-like strength. Joseph's brothers treated him unfairly because they were so jealous of him, but he revealed his strength and character by showing kindness to them.

Joseph's father, Jacob, had always showed partiality toward Joseph and his younger brother, Benjamin. They were the two sons he had with his favored wife Rachel, who died giving birth to Benjamin, which may have made the two boys especially close to his heart. Jacob's favoritism—which became obvious when he made Joseph a colorful coat—stirred up jealousy in Joseph's half brothers. To make matters worse, Joseph had a way of bragging on himself. He told his brothers about a dream he had in which all twelve sons were tying sheaves of grain; Joseph's sheaf stood up while his brothers' bowed down to it. In another dream, he saw the sun and moon and eleven stars bowing down to him. This time, even his father rebuked him. Outraged, his brothers asked, "Do you think we will bow down to you?" They were angry enough to kill him.

When Jacob sent Joseph to check on his brothers while they were tending the sheep, they spied an opportunity. All but his brother Reuben began scheming to kill him. Reuben succeeded in convincing them to leave Joseph in a well rather than shed any blood, and planned to come back later to rescue his brother. But while he was away, the others sold Joseph to a caravan of merchants traveling to Egypt. Imagine the young boy's cries of fear and hurt as the merchants bound and carried him away.

/// Mark Martin is a dedicated weightlifter and works out almost daily in a specially designed gym in his home near Daytona Beach, Florida. Although one of the circuit's oldest semi-regular competitors, he is one of the best conditioned.

Joseph, however, made the best of the situation. He trusted in God and remained faithful to Him even during trying circumstances in Egypt. After working for Potiphar, an Egyptian official, and quickly moving up the ranks to become his most trusted servant, Joseph lost everything and was thrown in prison because the man's wife wrongly accused him of taking advantage of her.

While in prison, Joseph interpreted the dreams of the king's former baker and cupbearer, and both men's dreams soon became reality. Years later, after he had been restored to his position in the king's court, the cupbearer remembered Joseph's gift when the king had a troubling dream. The king sent for Joseph, who interpreted his dream (while being careful to give God the credit). Joseph told the king that Egypt would experience seven years of plenty followed by seven years of severe famine. He suggested that the king store grain during the plentiful years and then distribute it when food supplies grew short. Pleased, the king made Joseph governor of Egypt.

After seven good years, famine indeed swept through Egypt and even reached Canaan, where Joseph's family lived. His brothers had to come to Egypt to buy grain—and there they met their long-lost brother. They didn't recognize Joseph and bowed low before him. But he recognized them and cried secretly.

A fool gives full vent to his anger, but a wise man keeps himself under control.

PROVERBS 29:11 NIV

EXPECT TURBULENCE

When others' lives disrupt our own with wrath, malice, or ill will, lean on Him who calms the storm.

Testing their behavior, Joseph accused them of being spies. In order to prove that they were honest citizens, he said, one of them must stay in Egypt until the others brought back their younger brother, Benjamin. Simeon stayed, and when Joseph's family finally relented and let Benjamin come, Joseph revealed his identity. Weeping, he said, "I am Joseph your brother, whom you sold into Egypt. But now, do not therefore be grieved or angry with yourselves because you sold me here; for God sent me before you to preserve life" (Genesis 45:4–5). With much joy, Joseph asked his brothers to bring his father and all their families to Egypt, where they would be spared and blessed.

Forgiveness for hurt and pain requires godly love and strength. Giants of faith like Joseph inspire us to respond to hurtful and unjust actions with humility and kindness. Are you nursing anger and ill will, or are you willing to let God soften your heart?

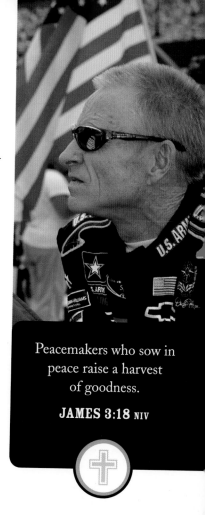

Peacemakers who sow in peace raise a harvest of goodness.

JAMES 3:18 NIV

LET US LEARN A LESSON FROM LITTLE CHILDREN—THEY FORGIVE SO EASILY.

We can get angry, but we don't have to stay angry.

CHAPTER nine

MAKING
THE TURN

Jeff Burton

// Auto racing is all about making tough decisions—

and making many of them in a split-second.

Drive into the pits now, or wait a few laps and hope for a caution flag? Try to make the winning pass in the first turn on the last lap, or wait until turn four? Follow the inside line of cars and hope it advances, or move to the outside line?

In a fifteen-year career in NASCAR Cup racing, Jeff Burton has had to make many hard choices. The toughest, though, came off the racetrack.

/// Burton owns an unusual NASCAR statistic. In 2000, he led every lap of a Cup race at New Hampshire International Speedway, becoming one of only a handful of drivers to so dominate an event in modern-day stock car racing.

PUSHING IT

When the race car won't move through the turns at high speeds, the driver and crew work with it to improve its "handling." Without God's leadership, it's tough to change your life's directions. ////

BURTON MADE HIS NAME AS ONE OF NASCAR'S TOP DRIVERS while racing for team owner Jack Roush. The two got together in 1996, Burton's third full season at the Cup level. Only one year later, Burton scored his first Cup victory (he won three times that season) and finished fourth in series points.

Over the next four years, Burton won a total of fifteen races and added points finishes of fifth (twice) and third to his resumé. Increasingly, journalists and fans were naming Burton as a favorite to win a Cup championship.

LORD, often we have doubted You when our way is difficult, but You are always faithful to Your promises. Plant Your word in our hearts and increase our faith so that many others may believe in You and be blessed. Amen.

Instead, Burton's career went into reverse. He won two races in 2001 but went winless over the next two seasons, and his points finishes dropped drastically—to tenth in 2001 and twelfth in 2002 and 2003.

Although Roush's abilities as the builder of strong teams were not in question, and Burton still enjoyed respect as a top-of-the-line driver, clearly something was amiss. Even the best team-driver lineups some-times struggle and lose their way, and the Burton-Roush story showed every indication of heading in that direction.

Burton could read the writing on the pit wall. He saw the need for a change, and, although it was tough to end his association with

> Trust in the LORD with all your heart,
>
> And lean not on your own understanding;
>
> In all your ways acknowledge Him,
>
> And He shall direct your paths.
>
> **PROVERBS 3:5-6**

/// Like many other racers, Burton got his start in go-karts. He won two Virginia state karting championships.

Roush after a very productive partnership, he decided to take a detour. Burton reached an agreement to drive for rival team owner Richard Childress, and the switch occurred in the middle of the 2004 season.

"They've all worked real hard with me, and I've worked real hard with them," Burton said of his crew as he left Roush. "We've been a group that would fight together. Anytime you walk out from something like that—you build allegiances and alliances, that's what this sport's about—it hurts."

The Childress racing operation had struggled to return to championship form after it lost top driver Dale Earnhardt Sr. in a fatal accident at Daytona International Speedway in 2001, and Childress saw Burton as a stable and smart driver who could help the team rebuild its foundation and work on its shortcomings. Burton also needed to re-energize his career, so the pairing made a lot of sense to both parties.

After a period of adjustment, Burton returned to winning form with Childress and again became a championship contender.

SOMETIMES GOD SURPRISES US

with an enormous challenge that changes our lives dramatically, but we must be willing to submit to God's call, regardless of how difficult the task may seem. God called Abraham at the age of seventy-five. He told him to leave his home and friends to travel to a country he'd never seen, a place that God would show him. God promised to bless him and make of him a great nation—through him all the nations of the Earth would be blessed.

Abraham was not a perfect man, but he believed what God told him and was willing to do whatever God asked. After Abraham traveled to Canaan, God assured him in a vision that He would give the land to his descendants, who would be as numerous as the stars. Abraham believed God—even though his wife, Sarah, was barren and well beyond childbearing years.

After living in Canaan for ten years, Sarah began to doubt that she could give Abraham a child. Impatient, she took matters into her own hands. She asked her husband to take Hagar, her handmaiden, who would bear them a child. Abraham listened to his wife and became the proud father of Ishmael.

The LORD shall preserve your going out and your coming in

From this time forth, and even forevermore.

PSALM 121:8

/// Jeff Burton won six races in 1999, one of the best individual driving performances in recent seasons.

The curves of life exert high forces of pressure, but in Christ we can experience His peace and guidance.

///HANDLING THE PRESSURE

When Abraham was ninety-nine years old, God told him that if he would serve Him faithfully, He would make a covenant with him and give him millions of descendants who would represent many nations. Then God repeated the promise, "I will give you a son from Sarah." To himself, Abraham laughed in disbelief as he thought of Sarah giving birth at ninety. He said to God, "Yes, bless Ishmael." But God insisted that Sarah would give birth to a son who would be Abraham's heir. God would bless Ishmael, too, but the promise would be fulfilled through Sarah's son.

God reassures us of His promises. He appeared to Abraham again one afternoon near his tent at a grove of trees. Three strangers mysteriously appeared, and Abraham welcomed them and asked Sarah to prepare them some bread. He gave them a meal of roasted meat and cheese, and while

he served them, they asked about Sarah. Then one of them foresaw, "I will surely return to you about this time next year, and Sarah your wife will have a son" (Genesis 18:10 NIV). Sarah, overhearing, laughed at the thought of childbearing in old age. Then the Lord questioned Sarah's laughter: "Is anything too hard for the LORD?" (Genesis 18:14).

One year later, Sarah gave birth to a baby boy. His father was one hundred years old. He named their son Isaac, meaning laughter.

As so many of us do when God answers a long-awaited prayer, Sarah marveled at the miracle, saying, "Who would have said to Abraham that Sarah would nurse a baby?" (Genesis 21:7 NLT). From Isaac, God birthed a nation. Through this nation, God sent His Son, Jesus, and through Jesus all nations are blessed, for by faith, all who believe in Him become the children of God. Some of God's greatest acts start in the unlikeliest of places. If we follow His direction for our lives, trusting Him even when the road looks difficult and confusing, we'll experience His blessing.

⚡ ALONG THE ROAD

WHEN GOD CHALLENGES US TO MAKE DIFFICULT TURNS IN LIFE, HE WILL HOLD US STEADY.

If God leads us in another direction, our faith will be tested, but He will help us be faithful.

Delight yourself also
in the LORD,

And He shall give you
the desires of your heart.

PSALM 37:4

CHAPTER ten

SURVIVING
THE DESERT

Jimmie Johnson

// On the way to a successful driving career in NASCAR,

Jimmie Johnson learned some of the tools of the trade in off-road racing. One thing he learned was that he didn't want to race off-road forever.

Off-road racing, one of the wackiest forms of motorsports, typically involves long-distance runs across deserts in conditions that are, suffice it to say, less than pleasant. Competitors tangle with dust storms, the occasional bandit, domestic cattle roaming across the course, and nighttime driving that can test the nerve of even the bravest adventurer. The most famous of the off-road races is the Baja 1000, a thousand-mile journey contested annually in the deserts of Mexico's Baja California peninsula.

You're almost there, keep up the faith, and avoid foolish mistakes.

JOHNSON COMPETED IN THE BAJA 1000 several times, most memorably in 1995, the year he decided that possibly other forms of racing would be more to his liking—and considerably safer.

Johnson went on to win six off-road racing championships. But not at Baja. In 1995, the nineteen-year-old fell asleep at the wheel about three-quarters through the event and had a dangerous crash. For much of the one-thousand-mile distance of the race, many drivers run by themselves and thus don't expect quick help if they have a problem. And Johnson wound up in precisely that position. He wasn't injured, but he was stranded in the desert for most of a day.

"I went off the road about three or four in the morning about 800 miles into the 1,000," he said. "By the time somebody got to me, it was a good day later. By the time I got back in a safe environment, it was two days later.

"I learned a lot sitting there thinking about the mistake I made. I really just fell asleep at the wheel. At that time, I was pretty aggressive and made some dumb mistakes. That one really woke me up.

"I had been driving over twenty hours and was trying to make it until the sun came up. Once you see the sunlight, it really helps you stay awake. It was in that last hour or two before the sun came up, and I was on a long gravel road and kind of did a head nod like you might do when you're driving down the street and you're tired. But this head nod was at a hundred miles an hour with a corner coming up, and the car went off the road and flipped off through the desert. It bruised us up and bent the cage of the truck."

/// Johnson has had remarkable success at Lowe's Motor Speedway in Charlotte. He won NASCAR's longest race, the Coca-Cola 600, at LMS three straight times—in 2003, 2004, and 2005.

Show Your marvelous loving kindness by Your right hand, O You who save those who put their trust in You.

PSALM 17:7

AND, BY THE WAY, IT JOLTED JOHNSON FROM HIS SLEEPY STATE.

Rescue crews eventually reached Johnson, welded the race vehicle together, and returned to race central.

Johnson had a lot of time to think while he waited in the desert. He decided to pursue other, arguably saner forms of racing and embarked on a course that eventually led him to NASCAR and to one of the sport's most successful teams—Hendrick Motorsports. There he soon drove to national championships.

He who heeds the word wisely will find good, And whoever trusts in the LORD, happy is he.

PROVERBS 16:20

/// Before scoring his first Cup championship in 2006, Jimmie Johnson finished as runner-up in the series twice—in 2003 and 2004.

BY GOD'S HAND, Moses had led the Israelites out of Egyptian bondage into the Sinai Desert. There they lived as tent dwellers, nomads in search of Canaan, God's promised land. But just when they reached the southern edge of their destination at Kadesh-Barnea, they rebelled against God. Because of their rebellion and lack of faith in Him, they wandered in the desert for forty more years. Of that generation, virtually all died except two great men of faith, Joshua and Caleb. And they entered the promised land.

Caleb and Joshua were two of the twelve men whom Moses sent to scout the hills of Canaan. After forty days, the spies returned with sweet pomegranates, figs, and a cluster of grapes so large two of them had to carry

rebelled against Your leadership. Forgive us and lead us by Your own hand out of our desert into Your good land. ////

it on a pole. The men said to Moses and the people, "We went to the land where you sent us. It truly flows with milk and honey, and this is its fruit" (Numbers 13:27). Despite this good news, however, the people grew fearful when, after showing them the fruit, the spies told them about the inhabitants of the land, how they were great giants who lived in fortified cities. Caleb tried to encourage them to have faith in God and to seize the land He was giving them. But the people refused to listen. They believed only the report of the other ten spies, who said that the Israelites would be like small grasshoppers before the great giants of Canaan who would devour them.

Then both Joshua and Caleb tore their clothes and begged the people not to rebel against God. They tried to persuade the people to trust in Him. But instead, the people discussed stoning Caleb and Joshua and choosing another leader to take them back to Egypt.

Meanwhile, Moses and his brother, Aaron, were in the tabernacle with their

Racing is not for the fearful; neither is the Christian life.

BEING//// ////BOLD

/// Many NASCAR drivers need dozens or even hundreds of races to reach victory lane for the first time. Johnson was a quick learner. He scored his first win at California Speedway in 2002 in only his thirteenth start.

faces to the ground praying to God, and He spoke to Moses concerning the congregation of Israel. The people still did not trust God, even though He had performed many miracles and signs before their eyes.

Furious because of their revolt and distrust, God would have destroyed them if Moses had not asked for mercy. In His grace and mercy, God said the people would continue to wander in the desert for forty years and die there without entering Canaan. Only their little ones and His faithful servants Joshua and Caleb would possess the promised land.

How often we, too, are so close to God's richest blessings, but we fail to trust His guidance and instead choose our own way. To experience the abundant life God offers us, we must remain faithful and surrender our lives to Him.

ALONG THE ROAD

TO FAIL TO FINISH A RACE IS DISCOURAGING, BUT WITH HELP FROM THE MASTER THERE IS HOPE FOR THE ONE AHEAD.

It is foolish to simply rely on our understanding when God has provided us a team of support.

NOT BY SIGHT

If we could see the smile God makes

When we with child-like faith, take

His hand and walk with Him,

We'd gladly obey and risk everything,

To enter His Promised Land.

POLLY HEMBREE

CHAPTER eleven

DOWN
BUT NOT OUT

Terry Labonte

// The results sheet from the 1982 Winston Western 500

NASCAR race at Riverside International Raceway, a defunct road course in California, lists driver Terry Labonte's reason for not finishing the race as "crash." That barely tells the story.

Labonte, who would go on to win two NASCAR Cup series championships, was only twenty-six on that November race day. Before the event ended, his career—and his life—were in jeopardy.

/// Terry Labonte owns one of NASCAR's most unusual records. He won Cup championships in 1984 and 1996. No other driver has won titles so far apart.

STICK WITH IT

Our spiritual traction becomes more difficult when we are suffering, but God will keep us on track.

LATE IN THE RACE, as Labonte entered the eighth turn on the long road course, near the end of a high-speed straightaway, his car apparently cut a tire. Helpless to control the vehicle, Labonte sailed at more than 180 miles an hour nearly head-on into the turn wall. His car launched into a series of rolls and finally came to rest on its roof.

"It's the fastest part of the track," Labonte said. "I thought, 'Man, I'm going to hit that wall.' But I don't remember hitting it. I was knocked out a good while, I guess. I remember having a hard time breathing when I came to. Then I saw all that blood. Mine."

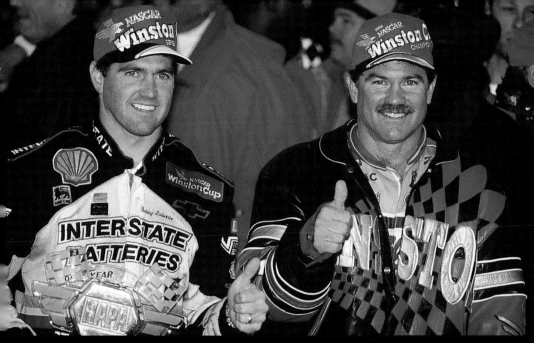

LORD, we pray for all those who suffer. We don't understand fully why people hurt. We do know You have promised to be with us through our trials. Your grace is sufficient to meet our needs. Grant us courage and the passion of Paul to let others know of Your love. Amen.

It didn't help that one of the first emergency workers Labonte saw when he regained consciousness was crying. He and many others who saw the wreck expected the worst.

Labonte's face suffered several deep cuts, requiring plastic surgery. He broke his right foot and left ankle and fractured several ribs, and was on crutches for weeks.

The only positive thing about the accident was that it occurred in the final race of the season, giving Labonte time to recover before the 1983 schedule started. Still, some wondered if Labonte would return to the racetrack that year—or ever.

/// In 1996, Labonte wrapped up the national championship in the last race of the season, and his younger brother, Bobby, emerged victorious in the finale, which was held at Atlanta Motor Speedway. They celebrated with side-by-side victory laps.

The accident, the worst of Labonte's long career, rattled him in more ways than one. He said he would have quit racing after the wreck if his wife, Kim, had asked.

"If she had come into the room and asked me to quit, I would have," Labonte said. "I would have regretted it later. But, if she had said anything, I would have quit. I was hurting that bad at the time."

But Labonte drove on—to twenty-two Cup victories, national championships in 1984 and 1996, and a selection as one of the top fifty drivers of NASCAR's first fifty years. He started 655 consecutive races, at that time a NASCAR record.

A bad wreck had knocked him down. But it wouldn't take him out.

....

PAUL THE APOSTLE, a giant of the New Testament, faced death and suffering constantly, yet remained faithful to his calling. He wrote, "We are hard pressed on every side, but not crushed; perplexed, but not in despair; persecuted, but not abandoned; struck down, but not destroyed" (2 Corinthians 4:8–9 NIV). More than anything else, he desired to share Christ with as many people as possible, regardless of the consequences.

> For I am persuaded that neither death nor life, nor angels nor principalities nor powers, nor things present nor things to come, nor height nor depth, nor any other created thing, shall be able to separate us from the love of God which is in Christ Jesus our LORD.
>
> **ROMANS 8:38-39**

Paul was a Roman citizen from Tarsus, an educated Jewish Pharisee, a tentmaker, and, later in life, an ambitious Christian missionary. Before his dramatic conversion to Christianity, he doggedly persecuted the early church, and he took great pride in his zeal as a Pharisee. But after becoming a follower of Christ, he no longer put merit in all his earthly titles and ambitions, humbly defining himself as the chief of sinners, captured by God's grace.

When given the opportunity, Paul eagerly shared his conversion experience with anyone who would listen.

With a party of men, Paul resolutely headed for Damascus to find Christians, intending to take them back to Jerusalem and throw them in prison for spreading what he believed to be heresy. But on the way, a dazzling, bright light surrounded him, and he fell to the ground.

A voice from the light asked, "Why are you persecuting Me?"

"Who are You, Lord?" Paul responded in awe.

The voice returned: "I am Jesus, whom you are persecuting. . . . Arise and go into the city, and you will be told what you must do" (Acts 9:4–6).

Be anxious for nothing, but in everything by prayer and supplication, with thanksgiving, let your requests be made known to God; and the peace of God, which surpasses all understanding, will guard your hearts and minds through Christ Jesus.

PHILIPPIANS 4:6-7

In our Christian walk we can expect to be misunderstood and misrepresented, but so was the Lord.

EXPECT TURBULENCE

/// During a long career that began in 1978, Labonte started 655 consecutive Cup races, giving him the nickname "Ironman."

Paul's stunned companions heard the voice but didn't see anyone. The brilliant light had blinded Paul, a condition that would last three days, so they led him into the city. There lived a faithful disciple named Ananias, and as Paul waited out his blindness, God appeared to Ananias and told him to go pray with Paul. Ananias balked—Paul's reputation for persecuting Christians was widespread. But God assured him that He had chosen Paul for a special purpose: to be His witness to kings, Gentiles, and Jews.

Ananias found Paul, and when he placed his hands on him, it seemed as though scales fell from his eyes, and he could see. He got up and was baptized, then spent several days with the disciples. Soon the former persecutor of the gospel began to astonish the people by boldly preaching Jesus as the Son of God. Doing so made him new enemies, and after a while, the Jews began plotting to kill him. But the disciples lowered him in a basket through an opening in the wall during the night so he could make an escape.

That night was the first of many brushes with danger. Preaching the forgiveness of sins and proclaiming Jesus as God's Son, the promised Messiah, Paul made three missionary journeys throughout the Roman Empire.

During those journeys, he was stripped and beaten, stoned and left for dead, shipwrecked, and imprisoned many times.

Through God's strength, Paul defied the obstacles, accomplishing a mission for which God had uniquely chosen him. While in prison, he wrote letters to various churches—epistles that today comprise much of the New Testament. Paul's letters have offered wisdom, encouragement, and comfort to Christians throughout the centuries. Just as importantly, Paul opened doors previously closed for Gentiles to embrace Christianity, working hard to convince Jewish Christians that God accepted the Gentiles and powerfully proclaiming the message of God's love to Jew and Gentile alike. Given his writings and his missionary efforts, it's clear that without Paul's sacrificial work, many in the Western world probably would never have heard the Gospel.

Paul's journeys sent him directly into danger and hardship—and eventually to his death. Yet he said, "But none of these things move me; nor do I count my life dear to myself, so that I may finish my race with joy, and the ministry which I received from the Lord Jesus, to testify to the gospel of the grace of God" (Acts 20:24). He would hold on to his mission, no matter what the cost. When we see our life as a mission from God and approach each obstacle with tenacity and perseverance, we find that even our worst sufferings can be fruitful in God's kingdom. We also find supernatural strength—and even joy—as we trust in and rely on God to help us accomplish His will.

ALONG THE ROAD

THROUGH HARDSHIP AND TRIALS OUR FAITH IS TESTED, AND WE BECOME STRONGER.

We pray not for suffering but for endurance.

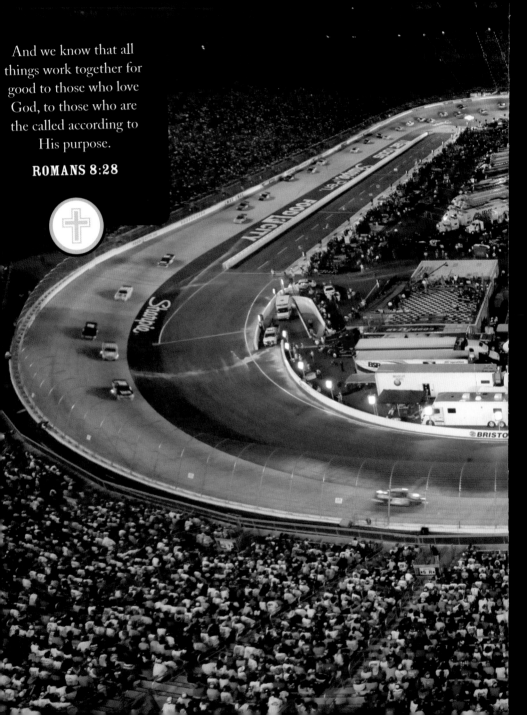

And we know that all things work together for good to those who love God, to those who are the called according to His purpose.

ROMANS 8:28

Ward Burton

CHAPTER twelve

IN THE WILDERNESS

// **Ward Burton** has enjoyed a successful NASCAR career, including a win in the Daytona 500, the sport's biggest race. But as a young man, Burton didn't really know which way to turn.

Part of a racing family (his younger brother, Jeff, is also a NASCAR winner), Burton grew up in South Boston, Virginia, and after high school attended Elon College near Burlington, North Carolina. But he was unhappy and unfulfilled there.

> The kingdoms of this world have become the kingdoms of our Lord and of His Christ, and He shall reign forever and ever!
>
> **REVELATION 11:15**

/// Three of Ward Burton's Cup victories came on two of NASCAR's most historic tracks—Darlington Raceway (two) and Daytona International Speedway (one).

"I CAME HOME (from college) one day, and I said, 'I think I'm going to major in philosophy,'" Burton said. "Mom and Dad told me I couldn't make a living on philosophy, that I had to take business and math. I took two business courses and flunked them. I got on my motorcycle and left and didn't ever go back."

Burton retreated to the forest along the Staunton River near his home. From a very young age, he had had a special place in his heart for the deep woods and the solitude they provided. There was a cabin in a far corner of the riverfront woods, and Burton spent many months there contemplating what to do next.

"I just didn't have a direction in my life," he said. "Didn't know what I wanted to do. I came back to what I did know."

He hunted and trapped and explored the woods, reacquainting himself with the land he had known so well as a small child. He had no human contact for months.

Eventually, Burton rejoined civilization with the intent of pursuing a racing career. With the support of his parents, he joined Jeff in competition at area short tracks and by 1995 had scored his first victory at NASCAR's top level. In 2002, he reached the peak of his sport by winning the Daytona 500.

> It is better to trust in the LORD
> Than to put confidence in man.
>
> **PSALM 118:8**

After he became a regular on the NASCAR tour and later one of its week-to-week victory threats, Burton didn't forget about the woods that had given him a refuge and a place to re-examine his life. He returned to those woods whenever possible, keeping alive his strong friendships with the property owners in the area. Late in life, two men who owned much of the property decided to give their holdings to Burton because they had confidence that he would protect their wooded acres.

"One of them said to me on his deathbed, 'Do what you said you were going to do and take care of my land,'" Burton said. "That's what we're doing."

Burton founded the Ward Burton Wildlife Foundation in 1996 with the idea of saving rural and forest lands from encroaching development. His major focus is a 1,123-acre tract he named the Cove. Located in Halifax County, Virginia, the Cove includes the deep woods where he roamed as a child and retreated as a young man.

Burton's work in conservation projects has earned him several national awards. Perhaps his greatest reward, however, came from the sense of direction the refuge gave him.

If we're not spending time in prayer and reflection, we're not going to handle well the uprising mishaps that come hurtling our way.

///HANDLING

FOR FOUR HUNDRED YEARS Israel had not heard the voice of a prophet. That silence was broken when John the Baptist emerged from the wilderness, with long hair and scruffy beard, dressed in camel's hair, crying at the top of his voice for the people to repent and be baptized.

Years earlier, the angel Gabriel had spoken to his father, Zechariah, with an amazing message. Even though Zechariah and his wife were without children and well past childbearing age, the angel told Zechariah that God had heard his prayers and would give them a son, who would be filled with God's Spirit before his birth. The angel said, "He will turn many of the children of Israel to the Lord their God. He will also go before Him in the spirit and power of Elijah . . . to make ready a people prepared for the Lord" (Luke 1:16–17). Not only would they have a child; they would have a son with an incredibly special mission.

After John grew up, he lived secluded in the wilderness, eating honey and locusts, spending time with God in prayer, and preparing his message of repentance. He believed that the Messiah would come soon, the One who would fulfill Isaiah's prophecy. John was to serve as God's messenger, one crying out from the wilderness for the people to repent and prepare their hearts for the coming of the Lord.

As an itinerant preacher proclaiming a message of repentance, John certainly drew crowds. Hordes of people from Jerusalem and Judea came to hear him preach on the banks of the Jordan River. He baptized those who repented of their sins and turned to God, reminding them that being a descendant of Abraham would not save them from God's judgment. He admonished them to live a changed life, to feed the hungry and clothe the poor. He advised the tax collectors who came to him to collect only what was required by law, and he warned the soldiers that they must be content with their wages and not take from others. Some of the religious rulers came, too, but John shouted at them to show evidence of their repentance because he knew that their hearts were far from God.

/// Ward Burton learned how to race at South Boston Speedway in Virginia, which is also the home track for his younger brother, Jeff.

DEAR LORD, thank You for brave men like John the Baptist. Give us repentant and receptive hearts, and help us to be bold through the power of Your Holy Spirit. May Your blessed Son rule our lives. In quiet solitude and prayer let us spend time with You so that You may accomplish Your mighty works of faith through us. Amen.

What percentage of our lives have we reserved for God—not for works or trying to please Him, but for Him alone?

////HANDLING

When Jesus came to be baptized, the Spirit of God revealed to John that Jesus was the promised Messiah. Feeling unworthy, John hesitated to baptize God's Son—"I need to be baptized by You, and are You coming to me?" But Jesus told him it was the right thing to do, and so John baptized Jesus in the Jordan. He had the privilege of being present—and even participating—when the Holy Spirit came upon Jesus like a dove.

Later John introduced Jesus to his followers as "the Lamb of God who takes away the sin of the world" (John 1:29). Earlier, he had told his disciples that one would come who was greater than he, for He existed long before him; he had baptized them with water, but the coming Messiah would baptize them with the Holy Spirit. Some of John's disciples then followed Jesus and became His disciples. Again God had used John to prepare people's hearts for Jesus and His ministry.

But even though John's outspokenness was an undeniable asset in his mission, it also got him into trouble. Reminiscent of the prophet Elijah of the Old Testament, who denounced King Ahab for his sins, John criticized King Herod for marrying his brother Phillip's wife, Herodias. Even though he respected John as a holy man, the king threw

BEHIND////
THE WHEEL

When our lives lack proper direction, let us trust Christ to steer our course.

him in prison to gain his wife's favor. While John was in prison, Herod tried to protect him, but Herodias tricked her husband into betraying John. After her daughter, Salome, dazzled Herod and his party guests with a seductive dance, he offered the girl by oath any gift she desired. Following her mother's prompting, Salome asked for John the Baptist's head on a platter, and Herod was forced to behead John or make a fool of himself in front of his guests. Like the prophets of old, John paid the ultimate price for his bold preaching.

When Jesus heard the news of John's death, He secluded Himself and prayed. His cousin had had a special place in His heart—He once told His disciples that no man born of woman was greater than John (Matthew 11:11).

We can learn many lessons from the life of John the Baptist. From his ministry, we learn that if we want God's approval, we, too, must humble ourselves, repent, and care for the needs of others. We learn that in Christ, we can live a Spirit-filled life, helping others to prepare for the coming of the Lord. We also learn that we shouldn't fear our desert experiences—God just might use a difficult or lonely time in our lives to teach us to depend on Him and to prepare us for a special purpose.

In Christ we can have peace, even in the most difficult circumstances.

////HANDLING

/// Although brothers Ward and Jeff Burton were raised together, they have dramatically different speaking accents. Ward's is a slow Virginia drawl; Jeff's is more mainstream. Jeff has often said there is a difference because "Ward was raised in the southernmost part of the house."

God looks down from heaven upon

the children of men,

To see if there are any who understand,

who seek God.

PSALM 53:2

CHAPTER thirteen

TAKE ACTION

Michael McDowell

// On April 5, 2008, Michael McDowell took the ride of his life—and not in a good way. It could have been his last ride.

McDowell, a promising rookie in NASCAR racing, was attempting to qualify his Toyota for the Cup race at Texas Motor Speedway, one of the fastest tracks on the circuit. Although almost all drivers try to post qualifying laps near the top of the list, it is particularly important for rookies to do well, both to secure a good starting spot in the race and to illustrate their talents.

A horse is a vain hope for safety;

Neither shall it deliver any by its great strength. . . .

Our soul waits for the LORD;

He is our help and our shield.

Psalm 33:17, 20

The LORD will preserve him and keep him alive, And he will be blessed on the earth.

PSALM 41:2

SO McDOWELL HAD A REALLY HOT LAP on his mind as he began his qualifying run. And there was another matter to consider. Before McDowell drove onto the track, driver David Gilliland's Ford had blown its engine, spraying oil on the racing surface. Safety workers put down an absorbent material to aid in the cleanup, a process that adds an element of the unknown to the track surface for the drivers who follow.

McDowell turned the first of two laps on the 1.5-mile track and later said he felt like his car was somewhat off in its handling. On the second lap, it was way, way off.

McDowell drove hard into the first turn on the second lap. Suddenly, he lost control, perhaps because of the material on the track, or perhaps because of excessive speed. In any case, the car shot into the outside wall at about 170 miles per hour, then launched into a series of ten barrel rolls down the track before coming to rest on its wheels. Fire erupted from the hood of the crumpled car at the end of one of the worst crashes in recent NASCAR history.

Remarkably, McDowell was not injured. He remained conscious throughout the accident and climbed out with only limited assistance from rescue workers. He later looked at his car—virtually destroyed—and shook his head in amazement that the crash hadn't ended more severely.

"FOR ME TO WALK AWAY FROM THAT WRECK IS UNBELIEVABLE," HE SAID.

McDowell's crash was the worst since NASCAR legend Dale Earnhardt Sr. was killed in a similar wreck at Daytona International Speedway in February 2001. After Earnhardt's death, a loss that shook the sport to its roots, NASCAR began a wide-ranging search for ways to make racing safer.

/// McDowell scored four victories in the Automobile Racing Club of America stock car series in 2007 and won the series' Rookie of the Year title. He also was second in championship points that season.

I will both lie down in peace, and sleep;
For You alone, O LORD, make me dwell in safety.

PSALM 4:8

so-called "soft walls" to the inside of speedway concrete walls. The walls, made principally of solid foam, eliminate some of the force of crashes. Drivers also are now required to wear head-and-neck restraints that limit the motion of the upper body in a head-on crash.

Thanks to those changes and others, McDowell left his race car only slightly dazed after a nasty crash.

....

PERSISTENT PRAYERS AND DECISIVE ACTION by God's servants often lead to safety and protection for others.

The Israelites returned to Jerusalem from Babylonian exile and found their city in shambles. Because the city's protective walls were demolished and the gates burned to cinders, the Israelites were defenseless and vulnerable to attacks by the surrounding nations. When Nehemiah, a cupbearer for Artaxerxes, the king of Persia, heard the plight of his fellow Jews, he responded with prayer and action to rebuild the walls and ensure the safety of the returning exiles living in Jerusalem.

Burdened for the exiles living in disgrace and danger, Nehemiah prayed and fasted before he asked the king for permission to journey to the land of his fathers to rebuild the city walls. God generously answered Nehemiah's prayers. The king not only granted his approval

DEAR LORD, forgive us for our apathy. Stir within us the spirit of love and concern for those with hurts and broken lives. Burden our hearts for our nation and our world. Thank You, Father, for the many years You have watched over us and kept us safe. In Your great mercy, continue to protect us from evil. Amen.

for the excursion, but also included an escort of army officers for protection and a few very important royal letters, one of which would instruct the manager of the king's forest to provide timber for the reconstruction. So Nehemiah set off to fulfill his dream of a restored Jerusalem.

Three days after Nehemiah reached the city, he and a few other men secretly inspected the broken walls and charred gates at nightfall. The next morning he assembled the people of Jerusalem and told them about all the king had done for him and how God's gracious hand was upon him. He rallied the people: "Come and let us build the wall of Jerusalem, that we may no longer be a reproach" (Nehemiah 2:17). It worked. His vision and passion inspired the exiles, and God's Spirit gave them a heart for the work.

But opposition came as soon as they began the rebuilding. Leaders of neighboring provinces did not want anyone helping these pitiful Jews—a sound wall around Jerusalem would be a threat to their power and secure positions. The enemies mocked and ridiculed the builders, teasing that even a fox couldn't walk across the wall without it collapsing. But Nehemiah rebuffed the scoffers, insisting that God would give the workers success.

> You are my hiding place, You shall preserve me from trouble;
>
> You shall surround me with songs of deliverance.
>
> **PSALM 32:7**

/// Michael McDowell took an unusual road to NASCAR, building his early success in open-wheel and sports car racing. He also was a national and international champion in kart racing.

> Blessed is he who
> considers the poor;
>
> The LORD will deliver
> him in time of trouble.
>
> The LORD will preserve
> him and keep him alive,
>
> And he will be blessed
> on the earth.
>
> **PSALM 41:1-2**

Rebuilding the wall was a national emergency, so Nehemiah had worked quickly to organize the reconstruction by assigning sections to the city officials, priests, residents, and specified families. Assorted groups were also assigned to repair the gates. Nehemiah worked with them and prayed for their protection and success, and soon the rebuilt wall reached half its height.

When the enemies saw the quick work the builders had done, they planned to attack the workers and kill them. Nehemiah encouraged the people, "Do not be afraid of them. Remember the Lord, great and awesome, and fight for your brethren, your sons, your daughters, your wives, and your houses" (Nehemiah 4:14). They would not only keep building, but fight to protect their efforts and their people.

The opposition realized their plan was foiled when Nehemiah armed the workers. Half the men worked while the other half stood guard, and a trumpeter stayed with Nehemiah to alert the others if fighting erupted anywhere along the expansive wall. They worked from daylight until the stars came out without so much as a pause, determined to build well and build quickly to protect the city.

Feeling defeated, their enemies turned to other tactics. They tried to intimidate, discredit, and ultimately kill Nehemiah. But he prayed for God's strength and protection to complete the great work God had called him to do. God was faithful, and in fifty-two days, the walls of Jerusalem were finished and fortified. The surrounding nations became afraid and lost confidence because they knew the Lord God was working on behalf of Israel. The wall served not only as a defense against enemies, but as a symbol of the power of God and what He can do with just one willing servant.

Our nation needs someone to care—someone who cares enough, as Nehemiah did, to not only fast and pray but also to respond to God's call for action. We each must ask ourselves what God would have us do to heal our broken nation and secure our walls. He's willing to act if we are.

Stop indulging yourself and help others get safely back on track.

PIT STOP

 **ALONG THE ROAD**

IT IS THE LORD WHO KEEPS US SAFE.

The effective, fervent prayer of a righteous man avails much.

JAMES 5:16

Kasey Kahne

CHAPTER fourteen

BEYOND
EXPECTATIONS

// When Kasey Kahne entered stock car racing, he had two tough acts to follow—Jeff Gordon and Tony Stewart.

Gordon entered NASCAR Cup racing in 1992 with a background of success in short-track open-wheel racing in midget and Silver Crown cars. Stewart arrived in 1999 with a similar resumé. Both zoomed to superstardom driving NASCAR stock cars, which are much bigger and heavier than the race vehicles they cut their teeth on.

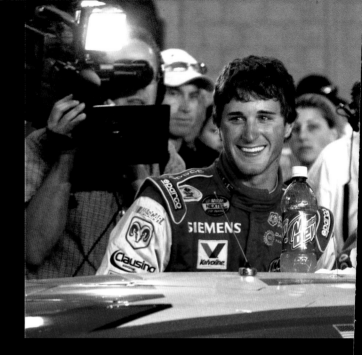

/// Kahne began building a foundation for racing success in 1996 at the age of sixteen by winning the Mini-Sprint championship at Hannigan Speedway in Washington.

When we are weak, by His grace, we are made strong. We can triumph!

GREEN LIGHT

/// Kahne's potential was realized in the 2006 season when he won six races, more than any other driver.

PRIOR TO THE APPEARANCE of Gordon and later Stewart, most successful stock car racers learned their trade on short dirt and asphalt tracks in stock cars. Gordon and Stewart set a new standard and opened a new avenue for entry into NASCAR. Their success prompted team owners to look toward young open-wheel aces for the next big star, the next Gordon or Stewart.

That brought Kasey Kahne onto the NASCAR stage. Kahne won the 2000 United States Auto Club midget championship as he made a name for himself in short-track open-wheel racing. In 2000 and 2001, he won the spotlighted "Night Before the 500"

> **LORD,** we are so overwhelmed with expectations from our families, our friends, our churches, and our employers. We are pressed on every side until sometimes we doubt our abilities and potential. Help us to seek to please You and commit our daily lives to You and Your work. When we do that, everything else will fall in its proper place, for You will bring inner peace and harmony to our lives. Amen.

midget race at O'Reilly Raceway Park near Indianapolis, a kind of lead-in to the Indianapolis 500. Gordon had won the same race in 1989 and 1990.

Kahne—young, handsome, and obviously talented—quickly moved onto the wanted list of NASCAR team owners. He jumped into NASCAR's No. 2 series in 2002 and then debuted in Cup racing with team owner Ray Evernham in 2004.

Almost immediately, because of the way he had duplicated the success of Gordon and Stewart in open-wheel cars, Kahne was expected

I have seen the God-given task with which the sons of men are to be occupied. He has made everything beautiful in its time.

ECCLESIASTES 3:10-11

When the competition is gaining and the crowds are relentless, the Lord can carry us to the finish line.

////HANDLING *THE*PRESSURE

/// Kasey Kahne is somewhat of a NASCAR oddity: he is a native of Enumclaw, Washington, an area that has produced very few NASCAR stars.

to shine in Cup racing. He was under the media microscope, and fans watched to see how quickly he could climb the ranks.

In his rookie season, he finished thirteenth in points, almost qualifying for the season-ending Chase for the Cup national championship run. He had five second-place finishes and won four pole positions. Not bad for a first-year racer.

"If you look at stock-car experience, I don't have a lot of that," Kahne said. "I have a ton of experience in sprint cars and midgets and dirt. I've done a lot of racing to be twenty-three years old."

Soon Kahne was putting his open-wheel experience to work. In 2005, he scored his first Cup victory, winning at Richmond International Raceway in Virginia. The next season, he solidified the "next big thing" talk that had surrounded him by scoring six victories and finishing eighth in the points race.

HE WAS ON HIS WAY.

PETER, JOHN, AND JAMES were Jesus' closest friends. They were privy to some amazing events that the other disciples did not see. For one, they saw Jesus transfigured before them on the mountain and even heard Him speak with Elijah and Moses concerning His death. Of all the people who followed Jesus, Peter, James, and John made up His inner circle.

> Let us throw off everything that hinders and the sin that so easily entangles, and let us run with perseverance the race marked out for us.
>
> **HEBREWS 12:1** NIV

Peter, however, stood out. Outspoken, bold, and confident—even brash—Peter was an exceptional disciple with great faith. He loved Jesus passionately and considered himself His most loyal disciple. He was the first to confess Jesus as the Messiah, the Son of God, and Jesus once said to him, "You are Peter, and on this rock I will build My church, and the gates of Hades shall not prevail against it" (Matthew 16:18). Jesus made it clear that He expected Peter to become a great spiritual leader.

But as ambitious as Peter was, and as high as Jesus set the bar for him, he had frailties just like our own. And just before Jesus' death, to Peter's shock and dismay, the Lord predicted Peter would even deny he ever knew Him.

"Simon, Simon!" He said. "Indeed, Satan has asked for you, that he may sift you as wheat. But I have prayed for you, that your faith should not fail; and when you have returned to Me, strengthen your brethren."

Peter protested, "Lord, I am ready to go with You, both to prison and to death."

But Jesus was insistent. "I tell you, Peter, the rooster shall not crow this day before you will deny three times that you know Me" (Luke 22:31–34).

That night in the garden of Gethsemane, Peter, defending Jesus, whacked off the ear of one of the armed men who came with Judas to arrest Him. In the melee that ensued, Jesus rebuked Peter and healed the man, and the other disciples ran away. Peter and John followed the soldiers and the captive Jesus to the house of Annas, the father-in-law of Caiaphas, the high priest. But Peter's apparent boldness would soon be tested.

John went inside the house and left Peter in the courtyard. As he warmed himself near a fire, a servant girl recognized him and said, "This man was with Him." But Peter denied it: "Woman, I do not know Him," he said (Luke 22:56–57).

Then another man identified Peter as one of the disciples, but he renounced the accusation. After yet another person recognized his Galilean accent and suggested that Peter must be a follower of Christ's, he angrily cursed and denied knowing Jesus. Just then, he heard a rooster crow, and he remembered Jesus' prediction that he would deny Him three times before the crow of the rooster. Filled with shame, Peter left and wept bitterly. Where would he go from here?

We all know what happened to Jesus after that—He was crucified and buried, and then He rose again. As for Peter, he was far from forgotten. After His resurrection, Jesus appeared to Peter alone. He loved Peter and wanted him to know he was forgiven.

Then, before He ascended into heaven, Jesus appeared to Peter and the disciples while they were fishing. As they talked with Him on the shore, He turned His attention to Peter.

Twice He asked Peter if he loved Him, and each time Peter said, "Yes, Lord." When Jesus asked a third time, Peter was grieved that He had to ask about his love so repeatedly, and he said humbly, "Lord, You know all things; You know that I love You" (John 21:17). And that was when Jesus commissioned Peter to be the shepherd of His sheep, their spiritual leader. Peter would not only be reinstated, but given the mantle Jesus had always meant for him to bear.

Later, after the Holy Spirit came with great power upon Peter and the disciples, Peter became the spiritual leader the Lord envisioned. He preached at Pentecost, and three thousand converts believed in Christ. As head of the early church, he strengthened and encouraged countless believers. In Jesus' name, he healed many with diseases and even raised Dorcas, a widow who helped the poor, from the dead. He may have stumbled in his path of discipleship, but by God's grace he went on to do God's will.

> But by the grace of God I am what I am, and His grace toward me was not in vain; but I labored more abundantly than they all, yet not I, but the grace of God which was with me.
>
> **1 CORINTHIANS 15:10**

In our fast-paced society, we often find ourselves serving in many roles, and it sometimes seems impossible to live up to the expectations of others. What we need to remember is that our only task is to please our Lord. When we recount the weaknesses of Peter and the magnitude of his life's work, we are humbled and awed by what God can do. We know God expects much of us, but by His Holy Spirit at work within us, He will achieve all that He has purposed for us to accomplish.

ALONG THE ROAD

WHEN WE HAVE AN ATTITUDE OF SERVICE WE CAN GO BEYOND WHAT IS EXPECTED.

Even the youths shall faint and be weary,

And the young men shall utterly fall,

But those who wait on the Lord

Shall renew their strength;

They shall mount up with wings like eagles,

They shall run and not be weary,

They shall walk and not faint.

ISAIAH 40:30-31

CHAPTER fifteen

ALL IN THE FAMILY

Kyle Petty

// Perhaps more than any other major sport, NASCAR racing is about families. Sons, grandsons, brothers, nephews, and even in-laws follow family members into racing, and names like Earnhardt, Pearson, Allison, Labonte, Baker, and Waltrip speak to the strength of families in the sport.

The name indisputably most identified with NASCAR, however, is Petty. From the sport's very beginnings, members of the Petty family have played significant roles in stock car racing, none more prominent than Richard Petty, the so-called "King" of NASCAR and the Cup series' all-time victory leader with two hundred wins to his credit.

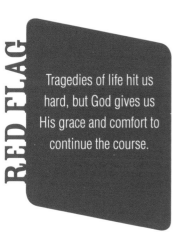

RED FLAG

Tragedies of life hit us hard, but God gives us His grace and comfort to continue the course.

THE PETTY RACING CONNECTION

began in 1949 with Lee Petty, Richard's father. One of NASCAR's pioneer drivers, Lee won three Cup series championships after starting a racing team in an old reaper shed on his farm in Level Cross, a small community in central North Carolina. Richard followed him into the driver's seat in 1958, and Richard's son, Kyle, ran his first race in 1979.

Adam Petty, the older son of Kyle and Pattie Petty, extended the Petty chain to four generations. He started racing in 1998 as an eighteen-year-old and, after achieving success in minor series, made his debut in the Cup series April 2, 2000, at Texas Motor Speedway. He thus became the first fourth-generation driver in NASCAR history. (In an ironic turn, Lee Petty, his great-grandfather, died of a stomach illness only three days after Adam's debut.)

The owner of the same bright smile and personality of his grandfather and father, Adam was expected to continue the Petty racing legacy well into another century. Tragically, he never got that chance. While practicing for a race at New Hampshire International Speedway on May 12, 2000, he was killed when his car failed to slow while entering a turn and slammed into the outside wall.

The tragedy stunned the Petty family and the entire NASCAR community. Lost was a precious son and a promising racer whose future appeared boundless.

Kyle and Pattie Petty struggled with the sudden loss of a young son (Adam was only nineteen) and began to look for positive

/// Kyle Petty scored his first Cup series victory in 1986 at Richmond International Raceway in Virginia. He thus became the first third-generation race winner in Cup history, joining his father, Richard, and his grandfather, Lee.

"Let the little children come to Me, and do not forbid them; for of such is the kingdom of God."

LUKE 18:16

CHECKERED FLAG

We are more than conquerors when we trust Christ to steer us through the victories as well as the hardships.

/// Kyle Petty's best seasons as a driver were 1992 and 1993. He finished fifth in Cup series points both seasons.

Therefore whoever humbles himself as this little child is the greatest in the kingdom of heaven. Whoever receives one little child like this in My name receives Me.

MATTHEW 18:4-5

ways to respond to their grief. They thought back to their son's experiences and how much he had enjoyed volunteering at a summer camp for chronically ill children. Adam had expressed an interest in starting such a camp, they said. So they made it their mission to make his idea a reality.

Later in 2000, the Pettys announced plans to build the Victory Junction Gang Camp on a seventy-two-acre site in Randleman, North Carolina, donated by Richard and Lynda Petty, Adam's grandparents. The camp, which opened in June 2004, serves children with chronic and serious medical issues who otherwise could not attend summer camp. The camp's facilities are specially designed for children who might have physical limitations, allowing them to swim, bowl, fish, and take part in other typical summer camp activities. And the centerpiece of the grounds is an activities building constructed in the shape of Adam's No. 45 race car.

The NASCAR community responded quickly to the Pettys' project. Donations from racing sponsors, drivers, teams, and fans poured in to aid in the construction and operation of the camp, and hundreds of children visit each year at no cost to their families. A second Victory Junction camp is planned in the Kansas City area, signaling that Adam's dream will continue to grow.

Kyle Petty wears a No. 45 cap in Adam's memory and also drives car No. 45 in the Cup series. Adam's greatest legacy, however, can be seen in the faces of the children whose lives are enhanced because Adam's family followed his dream.

> "And God will wipe away every tear from their eyes; there shall be no more death, nor sorrow, nor crying. There shall be no more pain, for the former things have passed away."
>
> **REVELATION 21:4**

....

WE ARE FILLED WITH JOY when God gives us children. From their infancy we adore them and respond fondly to their gentle coos and baby gibberish. We relish each stage of their development—the first smile, the first step, the first tooth.

We have great hopes and dreams for our children. And the loss of those dreams, the loss of a child, is devastating. The separation is painful, even unbearable—it's a hurt like no other. As the humble mother of Jesus, Mary experienced this very loss and pain.

Just as many loving parents savor the memories of their children, so did Mary. Luke tells us that when the shepherds bowed before Baby Jesus, telling about the angels' proclamation of Jesus' birth, Mary kept all of these sayings and "pondered them in her heart" (Luke 2:19). And she and Joseph marveled when Simeon, a devout follower of God, saw the baby Jesus in the temple and blessed Him, declaring that He was to be "a light to bring revelation to the Gentiles, And the glory of Your people Israel" (Luke 2:32). That moment must have been one of unforgettable awe.

Mary probably also vividly recalled the trip to the Passover feast when the child Jesus went missing. What worry and panic she and Joseph must have felt when they realized He was not traveling with their relatives as they had thought. They found Him sitting in the temple among the teachers, listening to them and asking questions. When His mother found Him and scolded Him for worrying them by disappearing, He merely said that they should have known He must be about His Father's business, a remark that surely lingered in Mary's heart.

According to the Scripture, Jesus "increased in wisdom and stature, and in favor with God and men" (Luke 2:52). A typical mom, Mary must have enjoyed Jesus' childhood, seeing Him grow and pleasing God and others. She knew this child was God's Son and was destined to do great things for His people.

And so Mary, a devout Jew and a regular worshiper at the temple, must have been deeply hurt and surprised when many of the religious leaders scorned Jesus and refused to accept her son's ministry. She no doubt delighted in His miracles of healing and reveled in the beautiful simplicity of His stories of the coming kingdom. Yet no one could prepare her for the reality of His cruel death on the cross.

What pain must have filled her heart as she knelt by the cross to be with Him at the hour of His death. Until He rose again, she would have to mourn the loss of a son felt by any mother who loses a child.

LORD, thank You for the joys of our family life, especially our children. Help us to trust You in all circumstances, even in the midst of pain and loss. We dedicate our lives to You. Use our resources as Your healing hands to touch and heal others who are suffering. Amen.

She could not have understood that the purpose of her son's death was to give eternal life to all who believe in Him.

Nor can we always understand why children suffer. Our children's pain is our pain, and it's as strong as any other hurt we'll encounter. But with God's help, we can minister to our families throughout all of life's peaks and valleys. And because of Jesus' death and resurrection, we can live in hope and seek to minister to those around us who are hurting even when we ourselves are hurt.

/// Kyle Petty was an exceptional high school athlete. He turned down several college football scholarship offers for a chance at racing.

"Let the little children

come to Me, and do not

forbid them; for of such

is the kingdom of God."

LUKE 18:16

Joey Logano

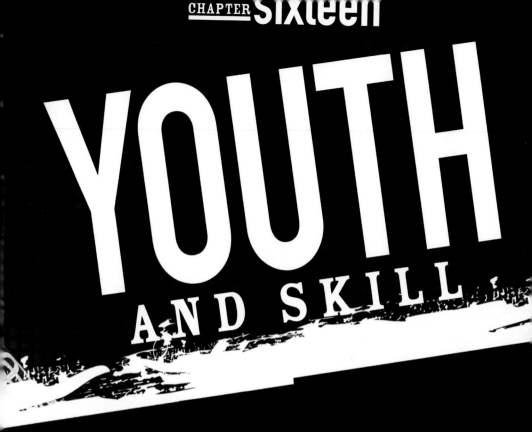

CHAPTER Sixteen

YOUTH
AND SKILL

// When race car driver Joey Logano was only fifteen years old, he received an amazing endorsement from Mark Martin, a veteran NASCAR driver.

"If I owned a NASCAR team and could do it, I'd put Joey Logano in a car right now," Martin said. "I am high on Joey Logano because I am absolutely, 100 percent positive that he can be one of the greatest that ever raced NASCAR. There's no doubt in my mind."

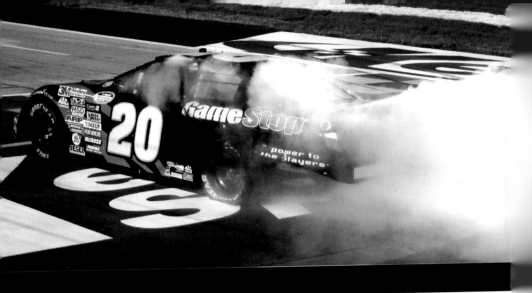

Equip and encourage the young at the start-finish line to run the race with faith and confidence.

/// At seventeen years old, Logano was featured in a "13 Young Stars" story in *Sports Illustrated*.

MARTIN MADE THESE STRONG STATEMENTS a full three years before Logano would even become eligible, at eighteen years old, to drive in a major NASCAR series. Martin's praise raised eyebrows here and there, but he repeated it often and with emphasis. He had seen Logano's strengths up close as Logano raced with Martin's teenage son, Matt, on short tracks in Florida.

Of all the young drivers racing at short tracks across the country, hundreds—perhaps thousands—could achieve success at the top rung of stock car racing if given the chance. There are just forty-three spots in

DEAR LORD, open our eyes and hearts to the great potential of our youth. Help us to lead them to You, and bless them with Your Holy Spirit. Make Your will known to them and empower them to walk the road of giants for the advancement of Your kingdom. Draw close to them so they may know Your infinite goodness and love for them, for to serve You is to live an abundant life. Amen.

each NASCAR Cup starting field, however, and only a limited number of openings each season. Additionally, many of those with great potential never get a shot at the brass ring because they can't make the right connections in a sport that increasingly demands fast results.

Logano benefited from his ties to Martin—and from a string of impressive accomplishments in his growing-up years.

Logano began his career in his native Connecticut in 1996 as a six-year-old. He started racing quarter-midget cars, and in 1997 he won the

CHECKERED FLAG

We rejoice to see our youth in God's victory lane.

Eastern Grand National championship. His family moved to Georgia a few years later, and Logano began a hot streak on southern tracks. His true potential began showing in 2005 as he won several races in the competitive United States Auto Racing Pro Cup Series—all this before he was old enough to get a regular driver's license.

By 2007, he was winning races in NASCAR's Camping World East Series, and he finished first in the prestigious Toyota All-Star Showdown at the fast and difficult Irwindale Speedway in California.

Logano turned eighteen on May 24, 2008, and became eligible for NASCAR's top three series. He immediately jumped into the No. 2 series—Nationwide—with the Joe Gibbs Racing team and, to the surprise of some, needed only three races to score his first win, which he earned at Kentucky Speedway. He thus became the youngest winner in series history.

Logano appears to have a limitless future in major-league auto racing. He's solid proof that youth isn't wasted on the young.

THERE'S SOMETHING TO BE SAID for the wisdom that comes with age. But youth has its virtues as well, and young Christians should never feel inferior to older, more experienced servants of Christ. Following Christ at an early age gives a person more time for service and intimacy with God—as Solomon advises the young: "Remember now your Creator in the days of your youth, Before the difficult days come" (Ecclesiastes 12:1). Young Christians can answer the call of God with vigor and vitality, while wise, mature Christians can exhort and encourage young believers.

The apostle Paul saw much potential in Timothy, a young convert from Paul's first missionary journey to Lystra in Lycaonia. Paul knew Timothy's grandmother, Lois, and mother, Eunice, who were both Jewish, and when Paul visited Lystra again on

> The glory of young men is their strength, And the splendor of old men is their gray head.
>
> **PROVERBS 20:29**

/// Joey Logano's career took a big step in 2005 when he was signed to a driver development contract with Joe Gibbs Racing, a NASCAR championship team.

> How can a young man cleanse his way? By taking heed according to Your word.
>
> **PSALM 119:9**

his second journey, Timothy and his mother and grandmother had all become respected members of the Christian congregation. Paul was so impressed with Timothy that he asked him to accompany him on the remainder of his missionary journey. Before they took off, Timothy demonstrated his bravery and allegiance to Christ when he submitted to Paul's request that he be circumcised. (Since his father was Greek, Timothy had not followed the traditional law of circumcision, and the Jews in the surrounding towns knew it; Paul thought circumcision would give Timothy better standing with the Jews to whom he would be ministering.) Timothy also showed bravery and faithfulness simply by going with Paul: he knew that the journey would be perilous, for on Paul's first journey to Lycaonia, he was stoned and left for dead.

Timothy had proved himself up to the challenge of missionary work, and although timid and somewhat sensitive to his youthfulness, he soon became Paul's devoted protégé. Paul even sent him as a special emissary to various churches. To the troubled Corinthians, he wrote, "If Timothy comes, see to it that he has nothing to fear while he is with you, for he is carrying on the work of

/// Logano picked up the nickname "Sliced Bread" after another driver teased that he was the "biggest thing since sliced bread."

the Lord, just as I am. No one, then, should refuse to accept him" (1 Corinthians 16:10–11 NIV). If nothing else, Timothy exhibited perseverance as a qualification for ministry.

In the final chapter of Hebrews, Paul rejoiced that Timothy had been released from prison, showing that Timothy, like his devoted mentor, endured persecution, but also like his mentor, he remained faithful to the proclamation of the gospel.

Timothy had other unique strengths as a leader, and Paul could trust him to deal with sensitive issues in the churches because of his pastoral concern and gentleness. While Paul was in prison, he wrote to the church at Philippi, "I trust in the Lord Jesus to send Timothy to you shortly, that I also may be encouraged when I know your state. For I have no one like-minded, who will sincerely care for your state. For all seek their own, not the things which are of Christ Jesus. But you know his proven character, that as a son with his father he served with me in the gospel" (Philippians 2:19–22). Paul had absolute confidence in Timothy's devotion and sincerity, for he had worked alongside him as a son with his father. Together, they experienced the joys and hardships of the ministry.

> O God, You have taught me from my youth; And to this day I declare Your wondrous works.
>
> **PSALM 71:17**

/// Joey Logano's career took a big step in 2005 when he was signed to a driver development contract with Joe Gibbs Racing, a NASCAR championship team.

During Paul's latter days in prison, he commissioned Timothy to pastor the young church in Ephesus. As Timothy stepped into the leadership role, Paul wrote him two pastoral letters to instruct, guide, and encourage him in his ministry. In the first letter, he tells Timothy, "Let no one despise your youth, but be an example to the believers in word, in conduct, in love, in spirit, in faith, in purity. Till I come, give attention to reading, to exhortation, to doctrine. Do not neglect the gift that is in you, which was given to you by prophecy with the laying on of the hands of the eldership" (1 Timothy 4:12–14). Paul knew that his ministry was ending, but he was confident God would continue His great work through his beloved Timothy.

Our youth are our most precious investment, and we must pass the torch of the gospel on to the next generation. God has special gifts in various fields of service and a great adventure awaiting those who are ready to submit their lives to Him. More experienced Christians have the grand privilege of leading and guiding them to answer the call of God in their lives. Regardless of our age, God challenges us to race with the giants.

> For You are my hope, O Lord God;
>
> You are my trust from my youth.
>
> By You I have been upheld from birth;
>
> You are He who took me out of my mother's womb.
>
> My praise shall be continually of You.

PSALM 71:5-6